A S I A N
MYTHOLOGY

ASIAN
MYTHOLOGY

MYTHS AND LEGENDS OF CHINA, JAPAN, THAILAND, MALAYSIA AND INDONESIA

RACHEL STORM

LORENZ BOOKS

First published in 2000 by
Lorenz Books

Lorenz Books is an
imprint of
Anness Publishing Ltd.
Hermes House
88-89 Blackfriars Road
London SE1 8HA

© Anness Publishing
Limited 2000

Published in the USA by
Lorenz Books
Anness Publishing Inc.,
27 West 20th Street
New York, NY 10011;
(800) 354-9657

This edition distributed in
Canada by
Raincoast Books
8680 Cambie Street
Vancouver
British Columbia
V6P 6M9

A CIP catalogue record for this
book is available from the British
Library

Publisher: Joanna Lorenz
Managing Editor: Helen Sudell
Project Editor: Emma Gray
Contributing Editor: Beverley Jollands
Editorial Assistant: Helen Marsh
Designer: Mario Bettella, Artmedia
Map Illustrator: Stephen Sweet
Picture Researcher: Adrian Bentley
Editorial Reader: Richard McGinlay
Production: Don Campaniello

Printed and bound in Singapore

Previously published as part of a larger
compendium, *The Encyclopedia of
Eastern Mythology*

1 3 5 7 9 10 8 6 4 2

Page 1: Fu Xi
Page 2: Hikohohodemi
Page 3: Guanyin
Page 4: Shen Non
Page 5: Dainichi-Nyorai

Publisher's Note
The entries in this book are all listed
alphabetically. Where more than one
name exists for a character the entry is
listed under the name used in the original country of origin for that particular
myth. Names in italic capital letters
indicate that that name has an individual entry. Special feature spreads
examine specific mythological themes
in more detail. If a character is included
in a special feature spread it is noted at
the end of their individual entry.

CONTENTS

INTRODUCTION 6

THE MYTHS AND LEGENDS 12

YIN AND YANG 24

CREATION MYTHS 34

THE EIGHT IMMORTALS 42

SHAMANS OF MONGOLIA 50

CHINESE DRAGONS 58

THE SHICHI FUKUJIN 66

DEMONS 74

CHINA'S SACRED PEAKS 82

FAMILY TREES 86

CHRONOLOGY 87

INDEX 92

INTRODUCTION

T HE GREAT WORLD religions founded in West and Central Asia gradually spread eastwards through trading connections, missionary activities and military conquests, until they encountered the ancient gods and goddesses of the Far East. To a greater or lesser extent, Hinduism, Buddhism and Islam all influenced the indigenous beliefs of East and South-east Asia. Rather than opposing the influx of new faiths, though, the host countries tended to make the encroaching deities their own, embracing them within their own mythologies by a process of adaptation and assimilation.

China, the so-called "Mother Civilization of East Asia", did not view the incoming gods and goddesses as a threat. For many centuries, the Chinese had remained sublimely unaware that any civilization to rival their own even existed outside Chinese territory. When new influences did finally begin to filter into China, the immensely stable structure of Chinese society meant that, rather than feeling threatened by outside beliefs, the Chinese were able to modify and absorb them while maintaining their own culture.

China has its origins in the second millennium BC, when the Shang kings founded a state along the banks of the Yellow River which formed the basis for all subsequent development. During the ancient Shang dynasty, numerous gods were venerated and ancestor worship was already in evidence. A dynasty of legendary rulers, including the great Shang Di, stretched far back in time and helped to strengthen the status of the living emperor. Worshipped as the ancestor of the dynasty, Shang Di came to have an important role in Chinese religious thought. The Zhou invaders, who overthrew the Shang dynasty in 1027 BC, worshipped a deity known as Tian, or "Heaven". The emperor, known as the "Son of Heaven", was considered to act as an intermediary between Tian and his people on earth.

In the sixth century BC, Confucianism emerged, although it was not until the Han

BUDDHA was widely venerated in China, especially during the Tang dynasty between the seventh and ninth centuries AD. Buddhism offered a consoling message about the transience of suffering and the possibility of eventual salvation. (BUDDHA PREACHING, BANNER FROM DUNUANG CAVES, CHINA, 8TH CENTURY AD.)

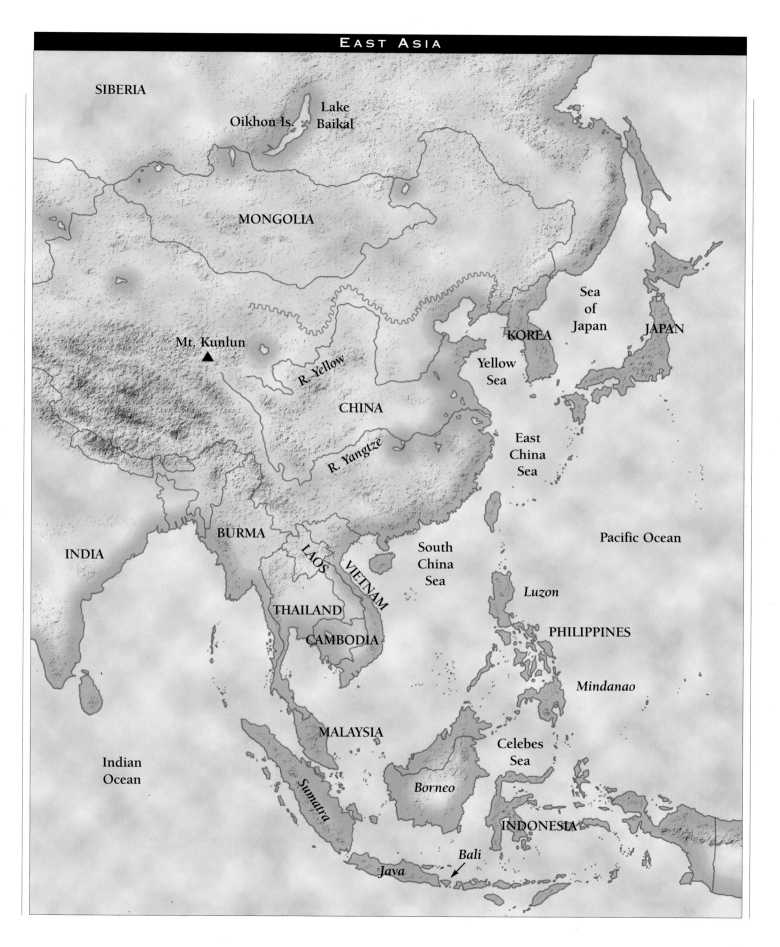

EAST ASIA

SIBERIA

Oikhon Is.   Lake Baikal

MONGOLIA

Mt. Kunlun

R. Yellow

CHINA

R. Yangtze

KOREA

Sea of Japan

JAPAN

Yellow Sea

East China Sea

Pacific Ocean

BURMA

INDIA

LAOS

VIETNAM

South China Sea

THAILAND

CAMBODIA

Luzon

PHILIPPINES

Mindanao

MALAYSIA

Celebes Sea

Indian Ocean

Sumatra

Borneo

INDONESIA

Bali

Java

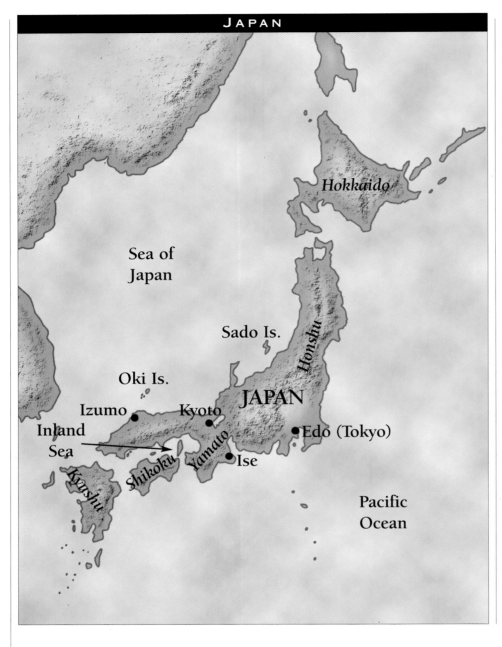

Sea of
Japan

Hokkaido

Sado Is.

Honshu

Oki Is.

JAPAN

Izumo
Inland
Sea

Kyoto

Edo (Tokyo)

Kyushu

Shikoku

Yamato

Ise

Pacific
Ocean

dynasty (206 BC–AD 220) that it was adopted as the philosophy of the state. Confucianism, the moral and political teaching of Kong Fuzi (551–479 BC), was developed during a period of violence and instability in China, and argued that human fulfilment was best achieved in a harmonious and highly structured society. It stressed the importance of respect for authority, filial piety and education. Kong Fuzi was, however, noncommittal about the existence of supernatural beings.

Whereas Confucianism drew its adherents from all social classes, Daoism, which emerged at about the same time, tended to appeal to the underprivileged. Its legendary founder, Laozi, was said to have been visited and consulted by Kong Fuzi. Daoists seek out the Dao, or "Way", a type of divine principle underlying nature. Its followers aim to achieve harmony with the principle by stilling and emptying the mind. Both a philosophical and a religious system, Daoism's religious aspect has a diverse history, interacting with popular Chinese religion. As a result, during the first millennium AD, it developed an elaborate pantheon of gods and goddesses, including the Xian, or immortals, beings who were not gods but had been granted eternal

YU HUANG (below), the "Jade Emperor", was the chief deity of the Daoist pantheon. His supremacy in heaven mirrored that of the emperor on earth, with whom he was said to correspond directly. (CHINESE WALL PAINTING, C. 1325.)

KONG FUZI is known in the West by the Latin rendering of his name, Confucius. Benevolence was central to his doctrine, which was adopted by the state during the Han dynasty. (CHINESE DRAWING.)

life and dwelt in a mythical land on earth. The emperor Qin Shihuangdi mounted an expedition to find this earthly paradise, and scholars laid down precepts that might be followed by the people during their quest for immortality.

The principal Daoist deity was the "Jade Emperor", who determined everything that happened in heaven and on earth. His heaven, precisely modelled on the court of the earthly emperor, contained a vast and complex bureaucracy, with numerous ministries and officials.

Around the beginning of the Christian era, Buddhism entered China, introduced by Buddhist monks travelling along the ancient trade route, known as the Silk Road, from India and Central Asia. It was a peaceful invasion, since Buddhism did not feel it necessary to reject the gods and spirits of popular religion, provided that people realized that only the Buddha could offer true salvation. In particular, the Mahayana school of Buddhism which arrived in China offered salvation to the broad mass of humanity, through the infinite compassion of the bodhisattvas. What made the incursion of Buddhism even smoother was the fact that the incoming religion had similarities with Daoism: both Buddhism and Daoism aimed to control mental processes and had interior enlightenment as their goal, rather than depending on the blessings of external deities. As a result, there came to be an interplay between the two faiths after Buddhism's arrival in China.

China had a widespread cultural influence on its neighbouring countries, including Japan. Shinto, the early religion of Japan, took much of its cosmology, including that of an egg-shaped cosmos, from Chinese sources. It also seems to have drawn on a variety of other ancient religious cults stemming from various parts of South-east Asia, with no fixed doctrine and no official sacred texts. Shinto's main objects of worship were the kami, shadowy deities who inhabited a world far removed from humanity but had control over human life, bestowing blessings if they were well treated and curses if they were offended or ignored. Whereas the Chinese regarded their "Jade Emperor" as a reflection of the earthly emperor, the Japanese claimed that the members of their imperial family were descended from their chief deity, the sun goddess Amaterasu, giving them a divine right to govern.

In the sixth century AD, Buddhism entered Japan, spreading from China and Korea. In spite of the profound differences between Buddhism and the indigenous religion, Japan adopted the new faith and made

SHAMANS of Mongolia perform ritual dances with the use of drums to induce a trance state. These charismatic figures have the power to control spirits and to make journeys out of their bodies to the upper and lower spirit worlds. They are central figures in many communities, combining the functions of priest and doctor. (ILLUSTRATION FROM LE TOUR DU MONDE. C. 1850.)

use of it to complement Shintoism. Buddhist icons were built in Shinto shrines, and the Japanese developed the doctrine that all kami were temporary manifestations of bodhisattvas. As a result, it still remains unclear whether some deities are Shinto or Buddhist. The overlap of Shinto and Buddhist ideas gave Japanese Buddhism its own distinctive flavour.

Korea's indigenous religion was based on shamanism, and elements of this remain today, in the mudangs, or female shamans who bestow blessings and tell fortunes. Buddhism began to dominate in 372, and achieved the height of its power after the unification of Korea under the Koryo dynasty in the 10th–14th centuries. As the state religion, Buddhist festivals became national holidays and all government officials were required to be proficient in Buddhist doctrine. The Korean Tripitaka was a major collection of

HUANG DI, the "Yellow Emperor" is revered as one of the founders of religious Daoism and the author of the first Chinese medical text. He is also said to have established China's social order by giving each Chinese family its name. As one of the five legendary emperors who rule the cardinal points, Huang Di presides over the centre.

Buddhist texts, and was completed in the 13th century. After the overthrow of the Koryo dynasty, the status of Korean Buddhism declined.

Chinese civilization also influenced South-east Asia, in particular Vietnam. Northern Vietnam had been incorporated into the Chinese empire in the third century BC, and did not regain its independence until 906. Even then, the first ruler Ngo Quyen modelled his new kingdom along Chinese lines. According to Vietnamese legend, the earliest rulers were descended from the dragon-lord Lac Long Quan, who came from the sea and taught the people how to grow rice. This myth also stated that the mother of the Lac lords of Vietnam was a Chinese queen.

SHEN NONG, one of the San Huang, or three legendary emperors of China, is said to have invented the plough and taught the skills of agriculture and forestry to the ancient Chinese. He also imparted the healing properties of plants, and is therefore regarded as the patron of pharmacists.

Burma, Thailand, Cambodia, Laos, Peninsular Malaysia and the Indonesian islands of Sumatra, Java and Bali were all affected by the advance of Indian rather than Chinese culture, and especially by the cults of the great Hindu gods Vishnu and Shiva. On the island of Bali, Shiva and Buddha were sometimes worshipped as a joint deity. From the beginning of the 17th century, Islam became the dominant religion of insular South-east Asia, carried there by Muslim traders. However, despite the impact of these major religions, indigenous beliefs persisted. For example, on Bali, where Hinduism is the

official religion, mediums still communicate with deities and spirits; among the peoples of Borneo the indigenous animistic beliefs still produce a mythology peopled by spirits connected with natural phenomena.

In other areas of East Asia, traditional beliefs have been lost under the force of incoming religions. Many of the shamanic myths of Mongolia were lost after the introduction of Buddhism to the country in the 13th century. In Siberia, shamanism came under threat from Muslim missionaries from the tenth century onwards. However, while Islam won many converts, a reverse process

became dominant in Japan in the 13th century, teaches that all of those who call on the Buddha in faith will gain entry to his wondrous paradise. By confidently looking forward to a glorious hereafter, Chinese and Japanese devotees came to view earthly life as simply transitory. The figure of Omito Fu/Amida thus demonstrates the manner in which an incoming deity can both be transformed by and, in turn, come to transform the society in which it makes its home.

MOMOTARO is a popular hero of Japanese folklore. Miraculously found as a baby inside a large peach, by an old couple who longed for a child, Momotaro grew up to be noble and brave, and freed the countryside from marauding devils with his trio of faithful animal companions, a dog, a monkey and a pheasant. (ILLUSTRATION FROM MYTHS AND LEGENDS OF JAPAN.)

also took place, with certain Central Asian Sufi orders being influenced by shamanism. Shamanism declined severely in the face of the missionary activity of the Russian orthodox church in the 19th century, and after the Russian revolution of 1917, Siberian shamans were persecuted by the Communists. Today, however, there are movements that aim to revive shamanism.

In general, the countries of East Asia have contributed to the already rich mythologies of the religions to which they have become hosts. In China, the goddess of mercy, Guanyin, evolved out of the Indian bodhisattva Avalokiteshvara and became a powerful mother goddess. Amitabha, the buddha of boundless light, became an important deity in both China and Japan. As Omito Fu in China and as Amida in Japan, he came to have an immense impact, in particular on the Japanese mind. Initially identified with the great Shinto goddess Amaterasu, Amida became the focus of the Pure Land school of Buddhism. Its doctrine, which

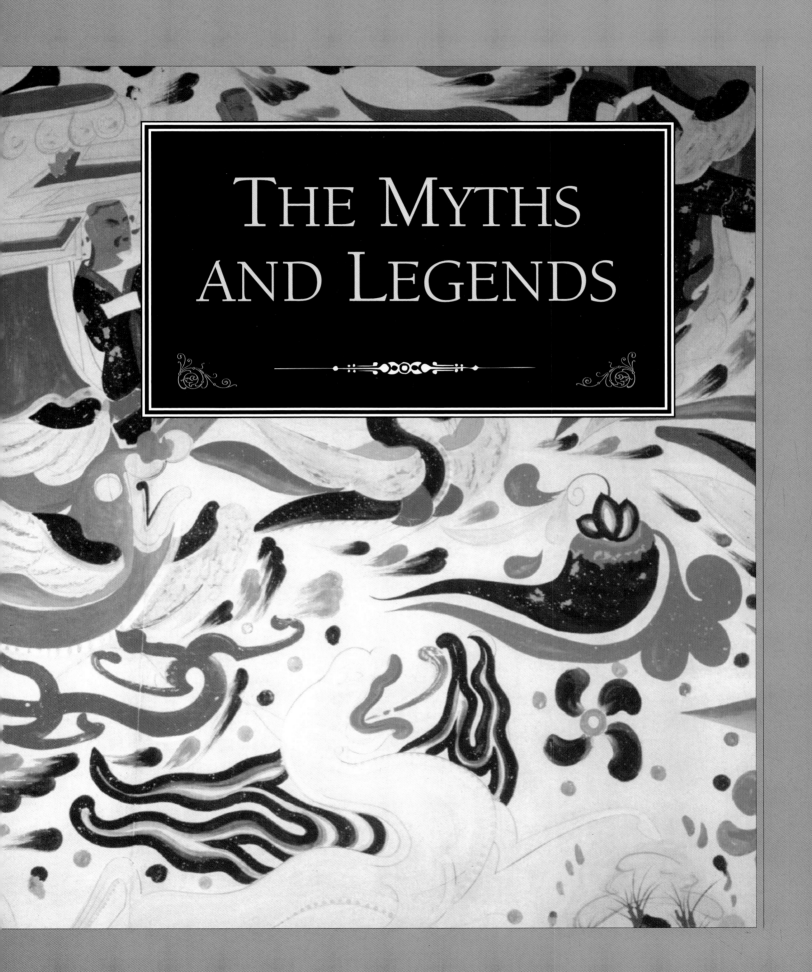

THE MYTHS
AND LEGENDS

A

THE ABAASY, according to the Yakut people of Siberia, are evil supernatural beings who live in the lower world and are ruled over by the malevolent spirit *ULU TOYO'N*. The son of the chief Abaasy is said to have only one eye and iron teeth.

AIZEN-MYOO is regarded as the god of love in popular Japanese belief. He is a deity of both physical and intellectual desire and represents love transformed through the desire for enlightenment. His body is red and he has six arms holding various weapons, three eyes and the head of a lion in his hair. Despite his frightening appearance, he shows great compassion for humankind.

AJYSYT see *ITCHITA*.

AMATERASU is the sun goddess of Japanese mythology and one of the most important deities within the Shinto pantheon. Her full name, Amaterasu-O-Mi-Kami, means "August Person who Makes the Heavens Shine". Amaterasu was brought into being when *IZANAGI*, the male half of the primal couple, washed his face after returning from *YOMI*, the land of the dead. The sun goddess emerged from Izanagi's left eye and the moon god *TSUKIYOMI* from his right. Izanagi told Amaterasu that she should rule the high plains of heaven and gave her his sacred bead necklace.

The storm god *SUSANO-WO*, who had been born from Izanagi's nose, angered his father by saying that, rather than rule over the waters as Izanagi had decreed, he wanted to join his mother *IZANAMI* in Yomi. As a result, Izanagi banished Susano-Wo. Before leaving, Susano-Wo said that he wanted to say goodbye to Amaterasu, his sister. However, Amaterasu suspected that her brother wanted to take her kingdom from her, so she prepared for battle. Arming herself with a bow and two quivers of arrows, she

shook her bow in challenge and stamped the earth beneath her feet. Susano-Wo claimed that he had no wish to usurp Amaterasu's power. Instead, he said that they could prove which of them was the most powerful by seeing who could produce male deities.

Amaterasu began the contest by breaking her brother's sword into three, chewing the pieces, then spitting them out. A mist appeared from her mouth, soon taking the form of three goddesses. Susano-Wo then took the fertility beads with which Amaterasu bound her hair and arms. He cracked the beads with his teeth, and from them produced five male gods. He then announced that he had won the contest. However, Amaterasu said that because the gods had

AIZEN-MYOO sits on a blossoming lotus, a symbol of enlightenment. He is popularly seen as the god of romantic and erotic love.
(JAPANESE SCULPTURE, C. 12TH CENTURY.)

come from her own jewels, she had won the contest. Susano-Wo ignored her protest and celebrated his victory by wreaking havoc on earth. He destroyed the rice fields, filled in the irrigation ditches and

AMATERASU (above), hearing the commotion outside her cave, looked out in curiosity and light returned to the world. (WOODBLOCK PRINT BY TAISO YOSHITOSHI, 1882.)

finished his rampage by skinning a young pony and hurling it through the roof of the sacred weaving hall, where Amaterasu and her attendants sat weaving. One of the maidens died of fright, and Amaterasu fled in terror and fury.

The goddess hid in a cave, thereby casting the world into darkness. The evil gods were delighted, as the darkness enabled them to perform their wicked deeds undetected. However, the good deities beseeched Amaterasu to return to the world. The goddess refused, and so the deities hatched a plot. They found the cock whose crow precedes the dawn and made a mirror strung with jewels. Then, after setting the cock and the mirror outside Amaterasu's hiding place, they asked the goddess *AME-NO-UZUME* to dance on an upturned tub. The cock began to crow and the goddess began to dance, her feet creating a frenzied drumming noise. Eventually, the goddess was carried away by the ecstasy of her dance and removed her clothes, whereupon all the gods began to laugh. Unable to contain her curiosity, Amaterasu emerged from the cave and caught sight of her reflection in the mirror. As she was lured out to gaze at her own beauty, the world was again lit by the sun.

Amaterasu and her attendants are said to have been weaving the garments of the gods, or those of the priestesses who officiate at ceremonies associated with the sun goddess's cult. Another theory argues that the women were weaving the fabric of the universe, which remained incomplete.

Until 1945, Amaterasu was worshipped as a sacred ancestor of the Japanese imperial family, and a mirror forms part of the imperial regalia. A major shrine to the goddess at Ise is visited by millions of pilgrims each year. (See also *CREATION MYTHS*)

AME-NO-UZUME, or simply Uzume, is the dawn goddess and the goddess of laughter, according to the Shinto mythology of Japan. She helped to tempt *AMATERASU* out of a cave after the sun deity, enraged by the behaviour of the storm god *SUSANO-WO*, had taken shelter there. Ame-No-Uzume danced at the entrance to the cave, eventually becoming so carried away by her antics that she flung off all her clothes. The assembled gods burst out laughing, and the disturbance caused Amaterasu to look out of her hiding-place to see what was happening. As a result, her light returned to the world.

Another myth tells how Ame-No-Uzume distracted a local solar deity, the "Monkey Prince", who had attempted to block the descent from heaven of *NINIGI* or Honinigi, Amaterasu's grandson. In due course, Ame-No-Uzume and the Monkey Prince were married.

AME-NO-UZUME (below) helped to lure Amaterasu out of a cave by arousing her curiosity with an erotic dance. (ILLUSTRATION FROM MYTHS AND LEGENDS OF JAPAN.)

B

AMIDA is a Japanese deity who derives from the buddha Amitabha, or "Boundless Light", who postponed his own entry into nirvana in order that he might save humankind. In China, Amida is known as Omito Fu. He is the central figure in the "Pure Land" sects of Buddhism. The devotees believe that, by invoking the buddha at the hour of their death, they may be reborn in the Pure Land, Amida's western paradise. Once in the Pure Land, the faithful remain free from pain and desire until the time for their final enlightenment arrives.

Amida was originally identified with *AMATERASU*, the sun goddess and the most important Shinto deity. He is often represented welcoming the faithful to his Pure Land, surrounded by numerous bodhisattvas and celestial beings.

ANTABOGA is the world serpent of Balinese mythology. At the beginning of time, only Antaboga existed. By means of meditation, the great serpent created the world turtle, *BEDAWANG*. Two snakes lie on top of the world turtle, as well as the Black Stone, which forms the lid of the underworld.

The underworld is ruled by the goddess *SETESUYARA* and the god *BATARA KALA*, who created the light and the earth. Above the earth lies a layer of water and, above the water, a series of skies. *SEMARA*, the god of love, lives in the floating sky, and above that lies the dark blue sky, home to the sun and moon. Next is the perfumed sky, which is full of beautiful flowers and is inhabited by Tjak, a bird with a human face; the serpent Taksaka; and a group of snakes known as the Awan, who appear as falling stars. The ancestors live in a flame-filled heaven above the perfumed heaven, and beyond that is the abode of the gods.

ARA is a spirit who features in a creation myth of the Iban, one of the Dayak peoples of Borneo. The

AMIDA sits on a lotus, emitting rays of golden light, with an aura larger than a billion worlds. (WOOD SCULPTURE, 18TH CENTURY.)

story tells how, at the beginning of time, Ara floated in the form of a bird above a boundless ocean together with another spirit, *IRIK*. The birds eventually plucked two enormous eggs from the water. From one of the eggs, Ara formed the sky, and from the other, Irik formed the earth. However, because the earth was too large for the sky, the two spirits had to squash it until it became the right size. During the process, mountains and valleys, rivers and streams were created. Plants began to appear, and then the two spirits decided to create human beings. At first they tried to make them from the sap of trees but, when this proved unsuccessful, they used the soil. After fashioning the first humans, they gave them life with their bird-song.

AS-IGA, according to the Ostyak people of Siberia, is a benevolent spirit. His name means "Old Man of the Ob", the great river that runs through Siberia.

THE BA XIAN, or Pa Hsien, or "Eight Immortals", are symbols of good luck and important figures within the Daoist mythology of China. They are not, however, gods, although they are often viewed as such. The Ba Xian are said to have achieved immortality through the practice of the Dao, or "Way". Although accounts of how

they became immortal did not appear until the 15th century, some of the Ba Xian featured in earlier myths.

The first figure to achieve immortality was Li Tieguai ("Li with the Iron Crutch"). An ascetic, Li Tieguai was taught by Laozi, said to be the founding father of Daoism, who descended from heaven in order to help him. One day, soon after gaining immortality, Li decided to visit a sacred mountain. He left his body behind, asking his disciple to look after it for seven days and telling him that, if by then he had not returned, the disciple was to burn it.

On the sixth day, the disciple's mother fell ill. Anxious to visit her, the disciple burned Li's body. When Li's soul returned, it found only a heap of ashes, and so entered the body of an ugly beggar with a crippled leg who had died of hunger. Although Li did not want to live in such a horrible body, Laozi persuaded him to do so and gave him a crutch to help him to walk. According to another tale, Li was given the crutch by *XI WANG MU*, the "Queen Mother of the West", who healed a wound on Li's leg and taught him how to become immortal. Li is usually depicted as a beggar leaning on an iron crutch.

Li Tieguai is said to have instructed Zhong-li Quan in the Daoist doctrine. According to one tradition, Zhong-li Quan found instructions for gaining immortality behind the wall of his dwelling when it collapsed one day. Zhong-li Quan followed the guidelines, whereupon he disappeared to the heavens on a cloud. Another tale tells how, during a famine, Zhong-li Quan miraculously produced silver coins and gave them to the poor, thereby saving them from starvation. Zhong-li Quan was fat, bald and sported a long beard. He was

THE BA XIAN included Zhang Guolao, who is represented here, riding his mule back-to-front, in a paper model outside a temple during a festival in Taiwan.

often represented with a fan made from feathers or palm leaves. After gaining immortality, he became a messenger of heaven.

Lu Dongbin was born in the tenth century AD. While still a student, he met a fire dragon who gave him a magic sword with which he could conceal himself in heaven. Later, Lu Dongbin visited an inn where he met a man called Han Zhongli. While Han Zhongli warmed up a pot of wine, Lu fell asleep and saw the whole of his future life in a dream. He dreamt that he would enjoy good fortune for 50 years but then his luck would run out, his family ruined and he himself killed by bandits.

When Lu Dongbin woke up, he became convinced of the worthlessness of earthly ambition and decided to renounce the world. He followed Han Zhongli into the mountains in order to seek the Dao and achieve immortality. Lu Dongbin is said to mingle with ordinary mortals, rewarding the good and punishing the wicked. He uses his sword to conquer ignorance, passion and aggression. He is the patriarch of many Chinese sects and the most popular immortal in Chinese culture.

Han Xiang is usually said to be a nephew of a Tang dynasty philosopher. He became a disciple of Lu Dongbin, who took Han to heaven and showed him the tree that bears the peaches of eternal life. Han began to climb the tree but slipped and crashed to earth. Just before landing, he achieved immortality. Han Xiang is said to have a wild temper and supernatural powers. On one occasion, he caused peonies to blossom in the middle of winter. A prophecy was written on their petals and, though at the time the words appeared to mean nothing, they later came true. Han is traditionally portrayed carrying a peach, a flute or a bouquet of flowers.

Cao Guojiu was a brother of Empress Cao of the Song dynasty. He lived in the 11th century AD and is said either to have become disillusioned by the corrupt life of the court or to have been overwhelmed with shame when his brother was found to be a murderer. Whatever the reason, he disappeared into the mountains in pursuit of the Dao.

On coming to a river, Cao tried to persuade the boatman to carry him across by showing him the golden tablet that had allowed him entrance to court. The boatman was unimpressed and Cao, ashamed, threw the tablet into the river. The boatman turned out to be Lu Dongbin in disguise. Lu Dongbin adopted Cao as his disciple and instructed him in the Dao.

Another version of the story tells how the emperor gave Cao a golden medal, which had the ability to allow its owner to overcome all obstacles. When Cao showed the medal to the boatman, a priest asked him why he found it necessary to use such methods of persuasion. Ashamed, Cao threw the medal into the river, whereupon the priest revealed himself as Lu Dongbin and promised to help Cao gain immortality.

Zhang Guolao was an old man who lived at the time of the Empress Wu of the Tang dynasty, in the eighth century AD. He is often shown riding back-to-front on a white mule. The mule was said to be capable of travelling thousands of miles each day and, when not being ridden, could be folded up and put in a bag. To bring the mule back to life, Zhang just sprinkled it with water.

The emperor grew intrigued by Zhang and asked a Daoist master to tell him his true identity. The master replied that he was afraid to answer the emperor's question because he had been told that if he did so, he would immediately die. He finally agreed to reveal who Zhang was, on condition that the emperor promised afterwards to go barefoot and bareheaded to Zhang and ask him to forgive the master for his betrayal. The emperor agreed, whereupon the master said that Zhang was an incarnation of the chaos that existed at the beginning of time. The master died, but when the emperor went to ask Zhang for forgiveness, he was brought back to life.

Zhang could endow the childless and the newly married with children. He is sometimes shown holding the peaches of eternal life or the bag that contains his mule.

Lan Caihe was either a girl or a man who looked like a woman. In summer she wore a thick overcoat and in winter only light clothing. She wore a belt made of black wood and a boot on only one foot. Her family dealt in medicinal herbs. One day, when she was collecting herbs, Lan Caihe met a beggar dressed in filthy rags, his body covered in boils. The girl looked after the beggar, who turned out to be Li Tieguai in disguise. For her kindness, Li Tieguai rewarded the girl with immortality. Lan Caihe then toured the country singing songs and urging people to seek the Dao. One day, she took off her coat, boot and belt, and rose into the sky riding on a crane. She is sometimes represented carrying a basket of fruit or flowers.

He Xiangu became immortal after grinding and eating a mother-of-pearl stone. After swallowing the stone, He Xiangu became as light as a feather and found that she was able to fly over the mountains gathering fruits and berries. One day the emperor summoned her to his court, but she became immortal and disappeared. She is usually depicted holding either a peach or a lotus blossom. (See also *THE EIGHT IMMORTALS*)

THE BAJANG is an evil spirit who, in the folk-tales of the Malay-speaking people of South-east Asia, appears when a disaster or illness is about to occur. He usually takes the form of a giant polecat (ferret) and is particularly harmful to children.

The master of the household is said to be able to catch the Bajang and keep him in a container. If the master feeds the Bajang milk and eggs, the spirit becomes friendly and will cause the master's enemies to fall ill. However, if the master fails to feed the spirit, he will attack him.

BARONG, according to Balinese mythology, is the leader of the forces of good and the enemy of *RANGDA*, the demon queen. He is regarded as the king of the spirits and traditionally takes the form of a lion. Ritual battles, usually ending in Rangda's defeat or a compromise, are staged between the two beings. (See also *DEMONS*)

BASUKI is a giant serpent of Balinese mythology. He lives in the underworld cave that is ruled over by the god *BATARA KALA* and the goddess *SETESUYARA*.

BATARA GURU is the name by which the Hindu god Shiva was known in South-east Asia before the arrival of Islam. He was the omnipotent sky god and was also viewed as a god of the ocean. Shiva was introduced to Java, Sumatra, Bali and the Malay peninsula sometime before the fifth century AD.

The Malay people added their own stories to the Indian tales of the great god's exploits. In Sumatra, for example, Batara Guru was said to have created the earth by sending a handful of soil to his daughter, *BORU DEAK PARUDJAR*, who had jumped from heaven into a vast ocean in order to avoid the unwelcome advances of the god Mangalabulan. A swallow told Batara Guru what had happened, and the god sent the bird down to earth with the soil. When the girl

BENKEI was the companion of the hero Yoshitsune. They were once attacked by a ghostly company of the Taira clan.
(*ILLUSTRATION FROM* MYTHS AND LEGENDS OF JAPAN.)

threw the soil into the water, it immediately formed an island. This

so annoyed the sea serpent *NAGA PADOHA* that he arched his back, causing the island to float away. Batara Guru then sent down more soil, as well as an incarnation of himself in the form of a hero. The hero managed to keep the serpent

still by placing an iron weight on his back so that he sank to the lower depths. Try as he might, Naga Padoha was unable to move the huge weight, but his writhings caused the formation of mountains and valleys.

After he had created the islands of the South-east Asian archipelago, Batara Guru sprinkled them with seeds, from which arose all animals and plants. Boru Deak Parudjar and the hero then produced the first human beings.

BATARA KALA, according to the creation myth of the Balinese, is the god who rules over the underworld cave together with the goddess SETESUYARA. Batara Kala created the light and the earth.

BEDAWANG is the Balinese world turtle whom the world serpent ANTABOGA created through meditation. Two snakes lie on top of the world turtle as well as the Black Stone, which forms the lid of the underworld. The god BATARA KALA and the goddess SETESUYARA rule over the underworld.

BENKEI, according to Japanese mythology, is the companion of the hero YOSHITSUNE. He is said to have been conceived by a TENGU, or demon. He soon grew to a great height and became very strong. None the less, Yoshitsune succeeded in overpowering Benkei in a duel, whereupon the giant became the hero's servant.

BENTEN, or Benzai, was one of the SHICHI FUKUJIN, or seven deities of good fortune or happiness, an assembly of immortals grouped together in the 17th century by a monk who intended them to symbolize the virtues of a man of his time. Benten was said to be the sister of the king of the Buddhist hells. Later, due to a mistake, she was attributed with the virtues of good luck and was included in the group of seven deities of happiness.

Benten helps human beings acquire material gains. She is said to have married a dragon in order to render him harmless, and is sometimes represented riding a dragon or sea serpent. She is associated with the sea. The goddess is

BENTEN holding a zither and riding on a dragon, is visited in her cave at Enoshima by a nobleman asking her to grant prosperity to his house. The goddess is associated with material wealth. (GOLD LACQUER SCREEN, 19TH CENTURY.)

also believed to be an exemplar of the feminine accomplishments, and she is often shown playing a musical instrument. Venerated by gamblers and jealous women, as well as by speculators and trades-

men, Benten is believed to bring good luck in marriage and is the patron saint of the geishas. (See also THE SHICHI FUKUJIN)

BENZAI see BENTEN.

BISHAMON

BISHAMON is a Japanese god who was derived from Vaishravana, one of the Guardian Kings of Buddhism. Bishamon, like Vaishravana, was originally the heavenly guardian of the north, but he later became the protector of the law who guarded people from illness and demons. He was also a god of war. Bishamon is believed to possess enormous wealth and to dispense ten sorts of treasure or good luck. As a result, he was included in the list of SHICHI FUKUJIN, the seven deities of happiness or good luck, an assembly of immortals grouped together in the 17th century by a monk who intended them to symbolize the virtues of a man of his time.

Bishamon is normally represented as a blue-faced warrior clad in full armour, and his attributes include a spear and a pagoda, a symbol of religious devotion. He is sometimes known by the name Bishamon-tenno or Bishamonten, and is often shown trampling two demons. In the sixth century, Prince Shotoku called upon the god to help him in his crusade against anti-Buddhist factions. (See also THE SHICHI FUKUJIN)

BORU DEAK PARUDJAR

BORU DEAK PARUDJAR, according to the mythology of Sumatra, is the daughter of the god BATARA GURU, the name by which the Hindu god Shiva was known in South-east Asia before the arrival of Islam. Batara Guru is said to have created the earth by sending a handful of soil to his daughter, Boru Deak Parudjar, who had jumped from heaven into a vast ocean in order to avoid the unwelcome advances of the god Mangalabulan. A swallow told Batara Guru what had happened, and the god sent the bird down to earth with the soil. When Boru Deak Parudjar threw the soil into the water, it immediately formed an island. This so annoyed the sea serpent NAGA PADOHA that he arched his back, making it float away.

Batara Guru then sent down more soil, as well as an incarnation of himself in the form of a hero. The hero managed to keep the serpent still by placing an iron weight on his back so that he sank to the depths. Try as he might, Naga Padoha was unable to move the weight, but his writhings caused the formation of mountains and valleys.

After he had created the islands of the South-east Asian archipelago, Batara Guru sprinkled them with seeds from which arose all the animals and plants. Boru Deak Parudjar and the hero then produced the first human beings.

BOTA ILI

BOTA ILI, according to the Kedang people of eastern Indonesia, was a wild woman who lived at the top of a mountain. Her

body was covered with hair, and she had long, pointed fingernails and toenails. She ate lizards and snakes and would cook them over a fire, which she lit by striking her bottom against a stone.

One day, a man called WATA RIAN noticed the smoke of Bota Ili's fire and set off to find its source. He took with him a fish to eat and some wine. When he reached the top of the mountain, Wata Rian climbed a tree and waited for Bota Ili to return with her catch of reptiles. The wild woman struck her bottom against a rock to start a fire, but to no effect. Looking up, she saw Wata Rian and shrieked at him to come down from the tree so that she could bite him to death. Wata

C

the god of wind. With their help he smothered Huang Di's soldiers in a thick, black fog, whereupon the latter invented the compass in order to find his whereabouts. Chiyou then called down the wind and rain, whereupon Huang Di summoned the goddess of drought, Ba, to clear the skies. Eventually, Chiyou was defeated and decapitated, although his headless body continued to run across the battlefield before finally falling down dead.

Chiyou was said to have invented warfare and weapons and was also a renowned dancer. Although his body was that of a human being, he had the feet of an ox. He was said to have four eyes and six arms, pointed horns, a head made from iron and hair as sharp as spears. He lived on a diet of sand and stones.

CH'IYU see *CHIYOU.*

CHORMUSTA see *QORMUSTA.*

CHU JONG see *ZHU RONG.*

THE CITY GOD was the impersonal tutelary deity of walled cities and towns, responsible to *YU HUANG,* the "Jade Emperor", in heaven. In each town, his temple was regarded as the "yamen", or celestial court, the counterpart to the terrestrial state yamen with its human mandarin responsible to the emperor in Beijing. The City God performed the same duties "on the other side", controlling harmful ghosts and spirits with his retinue of tamed demons within the city bounds. Prayers were addressed to him on behalf of a deceased, asking him to intercede with the ten judges of the purgatorial courts in the underworld, reflecting the widespread Buddhist concept of reincarnation.

Rian, unafraid, told her to calm herself or he would set his dog on her. The two of them lit a fire and cooked their food together.

Bota Ili drank so much wine that she fell asleep, whereupon Wata Rian shaved the hair from her body and discovered that she was really a woman. The two were eventually married.

BUJAEGN YED is a culture hero of the Chewong, a Malayan people. One day, Bujaegn Yed, a hunter, was eating the food he had caught when *YINLUGEN BUD,* an ancient spirit, appeared to him. The spirit warned the hero that he was committing a terrible sin in failing to share his food. Bujaegn Yed took

heed of the warning and took some of the food home to give to his wife, who was pregnant.

When Bujaegn Yed's wife was about to give birth, the hero was on the point of cutting open her stomach to allow the baby out, as was customary at that time, when Yinlugen Bud again appeared. The spirit showed Bujaegn Yed how to deliver a baby in the correct manner, and also taught him the rules and rituals of childbirth. Then, after teaching Bujaegn Yed's wife how to breastfeed a baby, the spirit disappeared. From that time on, women did not have to die when their children were born.

CAO GUOJIU see *BA XIAN.*

CHANG E see *ZHANG E.*

CHIYOU or Ch'iyu, is variously described as a son, descendant or minister of *SHEN NONG,* the ancient Chinese god, or culture hero, associated with medicine and agriculture. Chiyou rebelled against *HUANG DI,* the "Yellow Emperor", in a struggle for the succession. After Chiyou had driven Huang Di's forces on to an immense plain, the enemies engaged in a tremendous battle.

Huang Di's army was composed of bears, tigers and other ferocious animals, whereas Chiyou's army was composed of demons. Chiyou was also supported by Chi Song Zi, the "Master of Rain", and Fei Lian,

D

DAIKOKU was one of the *SHICHI FUKUJIN*, or seven gods of good fortune, a group of deities assembled in the 17th century by a monk who intended them to symbolize the virtues of a man of his time.

Daikoku was regarded as the god of wealth and a patron of farmers. He is often depicted standing or sitting on bales of rice, which are sometimes being eaten away by rats. Daikoku remains untroubled by the rats' greed because he is so wealthy. He usually carries a mallet, with which he is able to grant wishes. His picture was sometimes placed in kitchens, and he is sometimes said to have provided for the nourishment of priests. (See also *THE SHICHI FUKUJIN*)

DAINICHI-NYORAI is the Japanese form of the buddha Mahavairocana, or the "Great Illuminator". He was introduced to Japan at the beginning of the ninth century, together with numerous other Buddhist figures. He became the supreme deity of some esoteric sects and is sometimes regarded as the "Primordial Buddha". *YAKUSHI-NYORAI,* the divine healer, is sometimes seen as an aspect of Dainichi-Nyorai.

DAISHO-KANGITEN see *SHOTEN.*

DEMONG, according to the Iban of Borneo, governed the ancestors of the Iban people after they had been led from a country near Mecca to their present home. Demong married the daughter of a local ruler in order to ensure good relations with the existing inhabitants of Borneo. The woman, Rinda, had several children. When Demong was about to die, he ordered that a boundary stone be erected in order to mark the Ibans' territory. The stone stands to this day, and it is said that whoever attempts to move it risks incurring the wrath of Demong.

DIDIS MAHENDERA was a fabulous creature who, according to the Dayak people of Borneo, appeared together with *ROWANG RIWO* during the first epoch of creation, when a part of the universe was brought into being with each successive clash of the two cosmic mountains. The creature had eyes made from jewels.

DIMU see *DIYA.*

DIYA and Tian-Long were attendants of *WEN CHANG*, the Chinese god of literature. Diya, whose name means "Earthly Dumb", and Tian-Long, meaning "Heavenly Deaf", helped Wen Chang with the setting and marking of his examination papers, since, being deaf and dumb, they could be relied on not to leak the questions in advance. Another myth mentions these two as the primal couple, who gave rise to human beings and all other creatures. Diya was sometimes known as Dimu, meaning "Earth Mother".

DIZANG WANG, or *TI-TS'ANG WANG,* is one of the four great bodhisattvas ("buddhas-to-be") of Chinese buddhism. Long ago, Dizang Wang vowed that he would become a buddha, but only when he had liberated all creatures on earth from the relentless cycle of death and rebirth.

In one of his existences, he was a girl whose mother killed animals for food. Through meditating, the girl succeeded in saving her mother from hell. Dizang Wang is believed to succour all those who are detained in the courts of hell. He is depicted as a monk holding a metal staff which opens the gates of hell, and is often surrounded by the ten judges. He is the equivalent of the Indian bodhisattva Kshitigarbha and the Japanese *JIZO-BOSATZU.*

DONGYUE DADI, or Tung-yüeh Ta-ti, is the "Great Emperor of the Eastern Peak" according to Chinese mythology. He assists the "Jade Emperor" *YU HUANG* and supervises all areas of earthly life.

There are 75 departments within Dongyue Dadi's offices. One lays down the time for the births and deaths of all creatures, another determines people's social

DAIKOKU stands on two bulging bales of rice to symbolize his prosperity, and holds his magic mallet. As the patron of agriculture he was the protector of the soil and he was also seen as a friend of children. (JAPANESE SCULPTURE.)

E

standing, another their wealth and another the number of children they will have. Dongyue Dadi's offices are staffed by the souls of the dead. His daughter, Sheng Mu, looks after women and children. Dongyue Dadi is usually represented sitting down and wearing the garments of an emperor.

THE EARTH GOD, the ubiquitous local territorial deity, is the closest to the lives of villagers and is amongst those most frequently seen on the altars of the common people. The Earth God is not looked upon as powerful or fearsome. He is a celestial deity, the lowest ranking official in the bureaucracy of the celestial pantheon, and is the tutelary god of each sector of a large village or suburb; the protector of the well-being of both town and country dwellers. He has control over the wealth and fortune of the people.

The Earth God is almost universally thought to be an impersonal spirit. People appeal to him for anything that affects their lives and livelihoods. In times of peril, images of the Earth God have sometimes been taken from their shrines to be shown the cause of a problem, such as drought, flood, frost, caterpillars, locusts or mildew, to enable the deity to understand fully what his devotees are suffering.

EBISU, in Japanese mythology, was one of the *SHICHI FUKUJIN*, or seven gods of good fortune or happiness, an assembly of deities grouped together in the 17th century by a monk who intended them to symbolize the virtues of a man of his time. Ebisu himself is credited with the virtue of candour.

THE EARTH GOD (right) sits on the altar of a local temple, clutching his staff and tael of gold, symbolizing wealth.

DAINICHI-NYORAI (below), the "Great Sun Buddha", was the supreme deity of the Shingon sect. Its members held that the esoteric teachings of the Buddha were too obscure to be expressed in writing, but could be presented in painting. (PAINTING ON SILK, 13TH CENTURY.)

He is said to be the patron of labourers, wealth and prosperity, and to promote hard work. Ebisu is believed to have originated in Shinto belief as the son of *OKUNINUSHI*, the mythical hero. He is also sometimes identified with the third son of *IZANAGI AND IZANAMI*, the primal couple, and as such is regarded as one of the ancestors of the first people of Japan.

In some areas of Japan, the god of farms is called Ebisu; fishermen also invoke the god before going to sea. Ebisu is symbolized by a large stone, which a boy must retrieve from the bottom of the water. He is usually represented dressed as a peasant and smiling. He holds a fishing rod in one hand and a sea bream (sunfish), a symbol of good luck, in the other hand. (See also *THE SHICHI FUKUJIN*)

EC, according to the Yenisei people of Siberia, is the supreme god. He regularly descends to earth in order to ensure the well-being of creation. Ec drove his wife, *KHOSADAM*, out of the sky in punishment for being unfaithful to him with the moon.

THE EIGHT IMMORTALS see *BA XIAN*.

YIN AND YANG

DAOIST PHILOSOPHY CENTRED ON the principle of unity in the cosmos and the belief that a natural order, based on balance and harmony, determined the behaviour of everything in existence. Two interacting forces held the Chinese universe in delicate balance: yin, the female element, was associated with coldness, darkness, softness and the earth. It originally referred to the shady side of the mountain. Yang, the sunny side, was the male principle, associated with light, warmth, hardness and the heavens. The two forces were opposites but mutually dependent, and needed to be in equilibrium for harmony to exist. They were present in every aspect of the world, in contrasting pairs such as life and death, or good and evil, as well as in everyday activities, objects, animals and human characters. In the ancient Chinese creation myth, yin and yang were held inside the cosmic egg

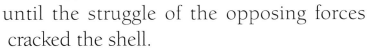

until the struggle of the opposing forces cracked the shell.

THE YIN/YANG SYMBOL (above) expresses the interaction between opposites that gives rise to the universe and everything in it. The dark section (yin) and the light section (yang) are directly opposed, yet interlocking and mutually dependent. Together they form a perfect circle. The two small spots show that each opposing force contains a small seed of the other within it. (CARVED CHINESE JOSS BOARD.)

THE BAGUA (left) were discovered by Fu Xi, the legendary emperor, who saw them inscribed on the back of a tortoise he found on the banks of the Yellow River in about 3000 BC. The constantly changing interactions of yin and yang gave rise to the infinite variety of patterns of life, symbolized in the three-line symbols of the eight trigrams. The top line of each trigram represents heaven, the bottom is earth and the middle line is humankind. (ILLUSTRATION FROM SUPERSTITIONS EN CHINE, 1915.)

THE YIN/YANG SYMBOL (below), surrounded by the trigrams of the bagua, was hung on the house door as a protective amulet to prevent the entry of devils. With it might hang a picture of the immortal Liu Hai with his three-legged bowl, who brought good luck to those involved in commercial ventures. He carried a string of gold pieces to remind him of a visiting philosopher who suggested he tried to pile eggs to demonstrate the precariousness of high office. (ILLUSTRATION FROM SUPERSTITIONS EN CHINE, 1915.)

THE PEI TOU IMMORTALS (above) were star spirits of which the most important were the "Three Stars of Happiness": Shou Lao, the god of longevity; Fu Shen, the god of luck; and Cai Shen, the god of wealth. They are shown here contemplating the yin/yang symbol on a scroll, and surrounded by symbolic figures of long life and immortality: the pine tree with Shou Lao's white crane, the stag and a child presenting a peach. (CHINESE SILK EMBROIDERY, 17TH CENTURY.)

THE DRAGON (right) and the phoenix were often used together decoratively. For the Chinese, dragons represented the male, yang element and were a beneficent force of nature, even though they had fiery tempers. The mythical phoenix represented the female, yin element. The dragon was the emblem of the Chinese emperor, and the phoenix of the empress, and together the two creatures were used to symbolize marital harmony. (JADE RITUAL DISC WITH DRAGON AND PHOENIX, C. 481–221 BC.)

F

EMMA-O (left), the king of hell, was no match for the strong man Asahina Saburo, and was humiliated by having to crawl between his legs. (KINJI INRO, 19TH CENTURY.)

EMMA-O (right) wears a magistrate's hat to indicate his office as judge of the dead. (NASHIJI INRO, 18TH CENTURY.)

EMMA-O, according to Japanese Buddhism, is the ruler of hell and the judge of the dead. He is identified with the Chinese deity *YANLUO WANG* and derives from the Hindu god of death, Yama.

Emma-O rules over the underground hell Jigoku, where he is surrounded by 18 generals and thousands of soldiers as well as demons and guards with horses' heads. The underworld is divided into eight hells of fire and eight of ice. According to one tradition, death begins as a journey across a vast, empty plain. In other versions of the tale, infernal beings guard the dead during their journey. At the entrance to hell lies a steep mountain, which the deceased have to climb before encountering, on the other side of the mountain, a river with three crossings. One of the crossings is a shallow ford, which those who have committed only minor sins may cross. Another is a bridge over which good people may pass. The third is a horrific torrent filled with monsters, through which evil sinners must struggle. At the other side of this third crossing waits a horrible old woman who strips her victims naked. They are then taken before Emma-O by the guards of hell. Emma-O judges only men; his sister decides the fate of women. The god sits between two severed heads, and a magic mirror reflects all the sinner's past wrongdoings. Emma-O then judges the individual's sins and allocates them to the appropriate hell. The souls of the dead can, however, be saved with the help of a bosatsu, the Japanese form of the bodhisattva.

ERLIK, according to the Altaic people of southern Siberia, is the king of the dead, an adversary of the supreme god, *ULGAN*. He incurred Ulgan's wrath by leading the first men to commit sin. The great sky god sent the saviour *MAIDERE* down to earth in order to teach men to respect and fear him, but Erlik succeeded in killing him. Flames shot forth from the saviour's blood, eventually reaching up to heaven and destroying Erlik and his followers. Erlik was then banished to the underworld. Erlik is regarded both as the first man and as the elder brother of the creator. He is depicted as a terrifying being, having taken on some of the characteristics of Yama, the Buddhist god of the underworld. He sometimes appears as a bear.

ES is the sky god of the Ket people of Siberia. Although he is invisible, he is depicted as an old man with a long black beard.

Es created the world and made the first human beings from clay. When he threw clay with his left hand towards the right, it became a woman; when he threw clay with his right hand towards the left, it became a man.

ESEGE MALAN TENGRI, or "Father Bald-head Tengri", is the sky god of the Buriat people of Siberia.

FANGCHANG see *PENGLAI.*

FU HSI see *FU XI*

FU XI, or Fu Hsi, according to Chinese mythology, is the brother and husband of *NU GUA*. Whereas Nu Gua rules over the earth, Fu Xi rules over the sky. They are both represented with the tails of dragons.

One popular myth tells how, long ago, a man was labouring in his fields when he heard a rumble of thunder. He ordered his son and daughter into his house, hung an iron cage under its eaves and stood in wait, holding a large iron fork. All at once, there was an enormous clap of thunder and a flash of lightning, and the monstrous thunder god, *LEI GONG,* appeared wielding a huge axe. The man attacked Lei Gong with his fork, pushed him into the iron cage and slammed the door shut. Immediately, the rain and wind ceased.

FU XI's (above) legacy to Chinese civilization included the invention of the calendar, the fishing net and the bagua, or eight trigrams. (19TH CENTURY ILLUSTRATION.)

The following morning, the man prepared to journey to the local market in order to buy spices with which to pickle the thunder god. Before leaving home, he warned his children not to give Lei Gong anything to eat or drink. As soon as the man had left, Lei Gong began to beg the children for just the merest drop of water. At first the children heeded their father's instructions, but eventually they relented. As soon as the water touched his lips, Lei Gong became strong again and burst out of his cage. Before leaving, he thanked the children for helping him and gave them one of his teeth, which he told them to plant in the ground. The children planted the tooth and, within a few hours, it grew into a plant bearing a gourd.

It began to rain, and by the time the man returned from market, the rain had covered the whole earth. The man told his children to climb inside the gourd for safety, then he built a boat and rose up to heaven on the swelling water. There, he knocked on the door and begged the lord of heaven to end the flood. The lord of heaven commanded the water god to put an end to the flood, but the god was so diligent that the water immediately subsided, and the man's boat crashed down to earth, killing him. However, the children were unharmed because the gourd cushioned their fall.

The children proved to be the only survivors of the flood. They became known as Fu Xi. When they grew up, the young man suggested that they have children. The young woman was reluctant, since they were brother and sister, but agreed on condition that her brother was able to catch her in a chase. Fu Xi caught his sister, and so began the custom of marriage. The woman then changed her name to Nu Gua.

According to another version of the tale, although the two beings wanted to marry and have children, they knew that they would first have to be granted permission from the gods because, being brother and sister, the marriage would be incestuous. The couple climbed a sacred mountain, and each built a bonfire on its summit. The smoke from the two fires mingled, and Nu Gua and Fu Xi took this to mean that they had been granted permission to marry. Time passed and eventually Nu Gua gave birth to a ball of flesh. Fu Xi chopped the ball into numerous pieces with an axe and carried the fragments up a ladder to heaven. A gust of wind scattered the pieces of flesh all over the earth; when they landed, they became human beings. In this way, the earth was repopulated. (See also CREATION MYTHS; YIN AND YANG)

FU XI (below centre) became the first of the legendary emperors of China, followed by Shen Nong and Huang Di.

FUDO-MYOO (left), a terrifying deity who protects Buddhism and its adherents, holds a sword in one hand and a rope in the other. (SCULPTURE, 12TH–14TH CENTURY.)

Fugen is often depicted sitting on a white elephant with six tusks, or sometimes riding four elephants. He may be shown with 20 arms.

FUKUROKUJU is one of the *SHICHI FUKUJIN,* the seven gods of good fortune or happiness, a group of deities assembled in the 17th century by a monk who intended them to symbolize the virtues of a man of his time.

Fukurokuju himself symbolizes the virtue of popularity as well as wisdom, longevity, virility and fertility. He is usually depicted with a very long, thin head to indicate his intelligence and a short, fat body. He is sometimes accompanied by a crane, a stag or tortoise, all creatures which symbolize longevity. Fukurokuju is of Chinese origin

FUDO-MYOO (above) is surrounded by a halo of flames, the symbol of his virtues. (PAINTING, C. 13TH CENTURY)

FUGEN-BOSATSU (below) sits on a lotus blossom carried by a white elephant. (JAPANESE SILK PAINTING, 14TH CENTURY)

FUDO-MYOO is the most important of the five great Japanese myoos, the equivalent of Indian Buddhism's vidyarajas, terrifying emanations of the five "Great Buddhas of Wisdom". Fudo-Myoo corresponds to the Buddha *DAINICHI-NYORAI.* He is usually portrayed with a terrifying face half-concealed by long hair and surrounded by a halo of flames. The flames are believed to consume the passions. In one hand, he holds a sword, which is used to conquer greed, anger and ignorance, and in the other hand he holds a rope with which he catches those who oppose the Buddha.

FUGEN-BOSATSU is the Japanese form of the bodhisattva or "buddha-to-be", Samantabhadra. He represents innate reason and is believed to be able to prolong people's lives. One tale tells how Fugen-Bosatsu appeared before a monk disguised as a courtesan with the intention of demonstrating that the nature of Buddha was latent in even the most sinful of women.

and may have been a Daoist sage. He is the godfather of *JUROJIN*, the god of longevity and happy old age. (See also *THE SHICHI FUKUJIN*)

FUXING see *SAN XING*

GAO YAO, or Ting-jian, was an ancient Chinese god of judgement. His accompanying animal, a mythical one-horned goat, helped him to detect injustice.

GIMOKODAN is the name that the Bagobo people of the Philippines give to the underworld. The Bagobo are a hill tribe living on the island of Mindanao. According to tradition, Gimokodan, the land of the dead, lies below the earth and is divided into two parts. One part is reserved for brave warriors who die in battle, the other part houses everyone else. A giantess lives in the second section and feeds the spirits of dead children with milk from her many breasts. Most of the spirits, however, turn to dew as soon as it is daylight and only become spirits again at night. A river lies at the entrance of Gimokodan, and all those who bathe in it forget their former lives.

GONG-GONG appears in Chinese mythology as a terrible monster who brings about a disastrous flood. He takes the form of a black dragon and is attended by a nine-headed snake. As the sworn enemy of the legendary benevolent emperor *YAO*, Gong-Gong decided to impale Mount Buzhou with his horn, thereby disturbing the balance of the earth and causing the rivers to overflow. He then tore a hole in the sky, disturbing the course of the sun. The monster is thus held responsible for all irregularities of weather and light.

According to another version of the tale, Gong-Gong and ZHU RONG, the divine lord of fire, decided to fight each other in order to determine which of them was the most powerful. The battle

GAO YAO's (above) *assistant in his pursuit of justice was a mythical one-horned animal, sometimes described as a qilin, or unicorn, who butted the guilty but spared the innocent.* (SINO-TIBETAN ENAMEL QILIN.)

continued for several days. Eventually, the two creatures fell out of heaven, and Gong-Gong was defeated. Gong-Gong was so humiliated by having lost the battle that he determined to kill himself by running head first at Mount Buzhou, one of the mountains which supported the sky. When Gong-Gong struck the mountain, a great chunk fell off, a huge hole was torn in the sky and enormous cracks appeared in the earth. Fire and water gushed out, and a massive flood covered almost the entire surface of the world. The few areas that escaped the flood were destroyed by fire.

The goddess *NU GUA* selected some coloured stones from the bed of a river and melted them down. She then patched the sky with the melted stones and propped up the four points of the compass with the legs of a tortoise. However, when Gong-Gong collided with the mountain, he caused the heavens to tilt towards the northwest, which is why all the great rivers of China flow eastwards.

FUKUROKUJU (left), *the god of long life and wisdom, is portrayed as a benevolent old man with an enormous brain.* (JAPANESE LACQUERED VASE, 19TH CENTURY)

GUAN DI *was worshipped as the protector of state officials in thousands of temples throughout China, in which the swords of public executioners were housed.*
(CHINESE PORCELAIN, 16–17TH CENTURY.)

Guanyin is believed to live on a mountain or an island in the Eastern Sea. She is said to have introduced humankind to the cultivation of rice, which she makes wholesome by filling each kernel with her own milk. The goddess comes to the aid of all those who need her help, especially when they are threatened by water, demons, fire or the sword. She is sometimes said to stand on a cliff in the middle of flaming waves and rescue shipwrecked people from the sea, the symbol of samsara, the ceaseless round of earthly existence.

The 14th-century novel *Journey to the West*, which is said to provide a popular record of Chinese mythology, tells how the "Monkey King" went up to heaven where he stole the peaches of immortality from the garden of *XI WANG MU*, the "Queen Mother of the West". The monkey incurred the wrath of all the gods and was finally taken captive by Buddha. However, Guanyin interceded on the monkey's behalf and he was allowed to accompany a Buddhist pilgrim during his journey to India.

Another myth tells how Guanyin was the third daughter of King Miao Zhong. She entered a religious order against the wishes of her father, who did all he could to persuade her to remain in the outside world. Eventually, the king decided that he would have to kill her. However, *YANLUO WANG*, lord of death, appeared and led Guanyin away to his underworld kingdom. There, Guanyin soothed the damned and transformed hell

GUAN DI is sometimes portrayed as a mandarin, sitting unarmed, stroking his beard. (SOAPSTONE FIGURE, 17–18TH CENTURY.)

GUAN DI, or Kuan-ti, is the Daoist patron deity of soldiers and policemen. He protects the realm and looks after state officials. During the Chinese Qing dynasty (1644–1912), Guan Di was venerated for his warlike functions. In other periods he was regarded as the guardian of righteousness who protects men from strife and evil. In popular belief, Guan Di was famed for casting out demons. He was also called upon to provide information about people who had died and to predict the future.

Guan Di was originally a general called Guan Gong, who lived in the third century AD, during a time of turmoil at the close of the Han dynasty. He was renowned for his military skill, but he also came to be admired for his great courage and loyalty, since he was eventually executed by his enemy as a prisoner of war because he refused to change his allegiance. Because of his many virtues he was later deified, being officially recognized as a god at the end of the 16th century. Guan Di is represented as a giant dressed in green with a long beard and a red face. He is often depicted standing next to his horse and clad in full armour.

GUANYIN, or Kuan Yin, is Chinese Buddhism's goddess of mercy or compassion. She developed from the male bodhisattva, or "buddha-to-be", valokiteshvara, known in Japan as *KWANNON*, and helps all beings on earth to attain enlightenment. Guanyin was herself originally regarded as male but increasingly gained female characteristics. Believed to bless women with children, she is sometimes depicted holding a child in her arms. However, she may also be represented as a bodhisattva with a thousand arms and a thousand eyes. She sometimes appears as a young woman holding a fish basket, standing on clouds or riding on a dragon in front of a waterfall.

GUANYIN (above), Chinese Buddhism's goddess of mercy and compassion, is often depicted holding a willow branch and a vase filled with the dew of compassion.

GUANYIN (right) helps all beings attain enlightenment. Originally a male deity, she increasingly gained female characteristics. (CHINESE PORCELAIN, 13–14TH CENTURY.)

into a paradise. Yanluo Wang then released Guanyin, and she was reborn on an island where she protected seafarers from storms. Her father then fell ill, and Guanyin healed him by cooking a piece of her own flesh for him to eat. In gratitude, the king ordered a statue of his daughter to be made. However, the sculptor misunderstood the king's instructions and made a statue with a thousand arms and a thousand eyes.

Guanyin is also credited with the ability to release prisoners from their chains, remove poison from snakes and deprive lightning of its power. She is believed to be capable of curing almost every sickness. A very popular goddess, her image is often found in people's homes and the festivals of her birth and enlightenment are endowed with great significance by Buddhists.

GUEI, or Kuei, according to Chinese mythology, are spirits formed from the *YIN*, or negative essence, of people's souls. These spirits or emanations are always feared because they are said to take their revenge on those people who ill-treated them when they were alive. They can be identified because they wear clothes which have no hems and their bodies cast no shadows.

H

HACHIMAN is the Japanese god of war. However, he is also a god of peace, and sometimes serves as a god of agriculture and protector of children. A historical figure, he is the deified form of the Emperor Ojin, who died at the end of the fourth century AD and was famed for his military deeds and bravery. Within the Shinto religion, Hachiman became a very popular deity, although his name does not appear in the sacred texts of Shintoism. He came to be regarded as a protector of Buddhism and is viewed by Buddhists as a bosatsu, the Japanese form of a bodhisattva, or "buddha-to-be". His sacred creature is the dove.

HAN XIANG see BA XIAN.

HE XIANGU see BA XIAN.

HIKOHOHODEMI is the great-grandson of the Japanese sun goddess AMATERASU and the son of NINIGI, or Honinigi, and his wife, Kono-Hana-Sakuyu-Hime.

Hikohohodemi's name means "Fireshade". His brother is called HONOSUSERI, or "Fireshine". Hikohohodemi hunted land animals, whereas his brother was a fisherman. One day the brothers tried to swap their means of livelihood but discovered that neither was able to perform the other's tasks. Honosuseri returned the bow, but Hikohohodemi had lost Honosuseri's fish hook and so offered him another in its stead. Honosuseri, however, refused to accept the replacement.

Upset, Hikohohodemi visited the sea god Watatsumi-No-Kami at the bottom of the ocean. Having previously found the fish hook in the mouth of a fish, the sea god returned it to Hikohohodemi. Meanwhile, Watatsumi-No-Kami's daughter had fallen in love with the young god. The couple were married and lived together for many years. Eventually, Hikohohodemi decided to return home. Before

leaving, Hikohohodemi's father-in-law gave him two jewels, which made the tide rise and fall; he also gave him a friendly crocodile to transport him on his journey.

Back on land, the god returned the fish hook to Honosuseri, who, despite this gesture, continued to pester his brother. Eventually, Hikohohodemi lost all patience and made the tide rise. When

Honosuseri was almost covered by the sea, he begged forgiveness and promised to serve Hikohohodemi, whereupon the latter caused the tide to go out.

The daughter of the sea god joined Hikohohodemi on land and announced that she was about to have his child. She made Hikohohodemi promise not to look at her while she gave birth,

HACHIMAN is the Japanese god of war, the deified form of the Emperor Ojin. Centuries after his death, a vision of a child appeared at his birthplace, identifying itself with an ideogram representing the name Hachiman. (STATUE BY KAIKEI, 13TH CENTURY.)

but the god was unable to resist the temptation and peeped through a crack in the wall of his wife's hut. There, he saw his wife transformed

into an enormous dragon. Afterwards, Hikohohodemi's wife returned to the sea and sent her sister to look after the child.

When the boy grew up, he married his aunt, the sea-god's daughter Tamayori-Hime, who had brought him up. They produced a son with two names, Toyo-Mike-Nu and Kamu-Yamato-Iware-Hiko. After his death, the boy was known as *JIMMU-TENNO*. He was the first emperor of Japan.

HINKON, according to the Tungu people of Siberia, is the god of hunting and lord of animals.

HKUN AI is a hero of Burmese mythology. He married a dragon who had taken the form of a beautiful woman. During each water festival, the woman became a dragon again, and Hkun Ai eventually became upset by his wife's metamorphoses. He decided to leave her, but before he did so, she gave him an egg. In due course the egg cracked open to reveal a son whom Hkun Ai called Tung Hkam.

When the boy grew up, he fell in love with a princess who lived on an island. Tung Hkam could not find a way to cross over the water to reach his beloved, until one day his mother appeared and formed a bridge with her back. Tung Hkam eventually became a great king.

HOMOSUBI see *KAGUTSUCHI*.

HONINIGI see *NINIGI*.

HIKOHOHODEMI was the grandfather of Jimmu-Tenno, the first emperor of Japan.

HONOSUSERI, according to the Shinto mythology of Japan, was the elder brother of *HIKOHOHODEMI*. Honosuseri was a great fisherman, while his brother hunted animals on land. Honosuseri's name means "Fireshine", and his brother's name means "Fireshade". The brothers are the great-grandsons of the sun goddess *AMATERASU* and the sons of *NINIGI*, or Honinigi, and his wife Kono-Hana-Sakuyu-Hime.

HOTEI is one of the *SHICHI FUKUJIN*, or seven Japanese gods of good fortune or happiness. He is represented as a Buddhist monk and is recognizable by his bald head and vast belly, a symbol both of his wealth and friendly nature and of a soul that has achieved serenity through Buddhism. Hotei is often shown leaning on a large sack, which is said to contain endless gifts for his followers. He is regarded as a friend of the weak and of children. He may have originated as a Chinese hermit called Budaishi who lived in the 10th century AD and was believed to be an incarnation of Maitreya. (See also *THE SHICHI FUKUJIN*)

HSI HO see *XI-HE*.

HSI WANG MU see *XI WANG MU*.

HSIEN see *XIAN*.

HSÜAN TSANG see *XUAN ZONG*.

HOTEI is depicted as a smiling monk with a large belly, which signifies contentment, not greed. He carries a fan and a sack. (IVORY NETSUKE, LATE 19TH CENTURY.)

CREATION MYTHS

MYTHS OF THE CREATION OF THE WORLD begin with emptiness, darkness, a floating, drifting lack of form or a fathomless expanse of water. Out of this dim swirl comes a more tangible object which holds the promise of both solid land and human life. The egg is a potent symbol of creation, and features in mythologies all over the world, including those of China and Southeast Asia. According to the folklore of the Iban in Borneo, the world began with two spirits floating like birds on the ocean, who created the earth and sky from two eggs. In Sumatra, a primordial blue chicken, Manuk Manuk, laid three eggs, from which hatched the gods who created the world. A Chinese creation myth, which may have originated in Thailand, begins with the duality governing the universe – yin and yang – struggling within the cosmic egg until it splits, and the deity Pangu emerges.

IZANAGI AND IZANAMI were the primal couple in the Japanese creation myth. The gods arose in a remote heaven far above the floating world, and generations of gods and goddesses were born before these two were instructed to complete and solidify the world below. As a result of their union Izanami gave birth to all the islands of Japan and numerous gods and goddesses, including the fire god Kagutsuchi who burnt her so badly that she died. These rocks off the Japanese coast, near Ise, are known as the Myoto-Iwa, or wedded rocks, and symbolize Izanagi and Izanami. They are bound together by a rice-straw rope.

PANGU (above) grew 3 metres (10 feet) every day, pushing the earth and sky apart. He lived for 18,000 years and when he died his body formed the world, each part becoming one of its elements. His flesh became the soil, his hair the vegetation, his perspiration the dew, and so on. Finally, the fleas and other parasites inhabiting his body became the first humans. He was said to be responsible for the weather: when he smiled the sun shone, but if he was sad or angry, storms would ensue. (LITHOGRAPH, 19TH CENTURY.)

AMATERASU (above) the sun goddess, was born from the left eye of Izanagi as he washed his face. The unruly behaviour of her brother, the storm god Susano-Wo, frightened and angered her so much that she hid in a cave, plunging the whole world into darkness. All the other gods assembled in front of the cave and lured her back out by showing her her own glorious reflection in a divine mirror. As she emerged, the sun reappeared. (UTAGAWA KUNISADA, THE GODDESS AMATERASU EMERGING FROM EARTH, WOODBLOCK PRINT, 1860.)

FU XI (top centre) was the creator god who figured in the oldest Chinese myths, but when legendary dynasties were devised in accounts of ancient history, he became the first emperor, and was said to have reigned from 2852–2737 BC. He taught his subjects how to make fishing nets and rear domestic animals, and discovered the bagua inscribed on the shell of a tortoise. These were the eight trigrams, based on combinations of the symbols for yin and yang, which formed the basis of Chinese calligraphy. (MA LIN, FU XI, 13TH CENTURY.)

SUSANO-WO (top right) was the storm god, the brother of Amaterasu. Sometimes known as the "Raging Male", he caused chaos in the world with his unpredictable behaviour, and the gods punished him by throwing him out of heaven. Once living on earth, his conduct improved, and he killed a terrible eight-headed serpent to win the hand of his beautiful wife, Kushi-Inada-Hime. While chopping through the serpent's tail, he discovered the legendary sword called Kusanagi, or "Grass Mower", which he sent to heaven as a gift for his sister.

HUANG DI, or Huang Ti, is the legendary "Yellow Emperor" of Chinese mythology who is said to have lived in the 3rd millennium BC. According to one story, Huang Di came into being when the energies that instigated the beginning of the world merged with one another, and created human beings by placing earthen statues at the cardinal points of the world and leaving them exposed for 300 years. During that time, the statues became filled with the breath of creation and eventually began to move. Huang Di allegedly received his magical powers when he was 100 years old. He achieved immortality and, riding a dragon, rose to heaven where he became one of the five mythological emperors who rule over the cardinal points. Huang Di himself rules over the fifth cardinal point, the centre. (See also *CHINA'S SACRED PEAKS*)

HUANG TI see *HUANG DI.*

IDA-TEN, according to Japanese mythology, is a god who protects monks and is the guardian of their

HUANG-DI is worshipped as one of the founders of Chinese culture and is said to have invented writing, the compass and the pottery wheel, and instituted the breeding of silkworms.

good conduct. He is depicted as a young man wearing armour and holding a sword. Ida-Ten is the Japanese equivalent of the Hindu warrior god Skanda, or Karttikeya, and was adopted by Buddhism in the seventh century.

ILA-ILAI LANGIT is a mythical fish who features in the creation story of the Dayak people of Borneo. The tale tells how, at the beginning of time, all creation was enclosed in the mouth of a gigantic snake. Eventually, a gold mountain arose and became home to the supreme god of the upper region, while a jewel mountain arose and became home to the supreme god of the lower region. The two mountains collided together on numerous occasions, each time creating part of the universe. This period has become known as the first epoch of cre-

ation, when the clouds, the sky, the mountains, the cliffs, the sun and moon were made. Afterwards, the "Hawk of Heaven" and the great fish Ila-Ilai Langit were brought into being, followed by two fabu-

lous creatures: *DIDIS MAHENDERA*, who had eyes made of jewels, and *ROWANG RIWO*, who had golden saliva. Finally, the golden headdress of the god *MAHATALA* appeared.

In the second epoch of creation, *JATA*, the divine maiden, created the land. Soon afterwards, hills and rivers were formed. In the third epoch of creation, the tree of life appeared and united the upper and lower worlds.

INARI is the god of rice, according to the Shinto mythology of Japan. His cult is extremely widespread since he is believed to ensure an abundant rice harvest and therefore brings prosperity.

In popular belief, Inari is represented as an old, bearded man sitting on a sack of rice, but the deity also appears in female form, with flowing hair. He, or she, is accompanied by two foxes. It is sometimes said that the god lives

HUANG DI (far left) was the third of the legendary emperors described in the Han dynasty to explain early Chinese history. Fu Xi and Shen Nong preceded him.

INARI's shrine at Kobe. Inari was the god of rice and is sometimes referred to as the god of food. He came to be regarded as a god of prosperity and is invoked by tradespeople. (THE SHRINE OF INARI AT KOBE BY WALTER TYNDALE, CANVAS, C. 1910.)

in the distant mountains and that the foxes act as his messengers. Alternatively, the god himself is occasionally regarded as a fox. Images of foxes are found in front of all of his shrines. Inari's wife was the food goddess *UKE-MOCHI*. When *SUSANO-WO* or, according to some versions of the myth, *TSUKIYOMI,* killed Uke-Mochi for producing food from her orifices, Inari took over her role as the deity of agriculture.

IRIK is a spirit who features in a creation myth of the Iban, one of the Dayak peoples of Borneo. Together with another spirit, *ARA,* Irik floated in the form of a bird above a boundless ocean. The birds eventually plucked two enormous eggs from the water. From one of the eggs, Irik formed the earth and from the other, Ara formed the sky. However, because the earth was too large for the sky, the two spirits had to squash it until it was the right size. During the process, mountains and valleys, rivers and streams were created. Immediately, plants began to appear. The two spirits then decided to create human beings. At first they tried to make them from the sap of trees, but, when this proved unsuccessful, they used the soil. After fashioning the first humans, they gave them life with their bird-song.

ISSUN BOSHI is a diminutive hero of Japanese mythology whose name means "Little One-Inch". His parents, despite being married for many years, had failed to conceive a child. In desperation, they prayed that they might be given a son even if he were only as tall as a fingertip. The gods took the couple literally and gave them a tiny child.

When Issun Boshi was 15 years old, he set off for Kyoto, taking with him a rice bowl, a pair of chopsticks and a needle stuck in a bamboo sheath. He paddled down the river, using the rice bowl as a boat and the chopsticks as oars. After arriving at Kyoto, Issun Boshi secured a job in the service of a noble family. For many years, he worked hard and his employers were pleased with him.

One day, the young hero accompanied the daughter of the house to the temple. On the way there, two giant *ONI*, horned devils, jumped out at them. Issun Boshi immediately attracted their attention so that the daughter could escape. One of the oni succeeded in swallowing Issun Boshi. Undeterred, the tiny man drew his needle out of its sheath and stabbed the devil in the stomach. As he crawled up the devil's throat, he continued to stab him until, with huge relief, the oni spat him out. Immediately, the other oni pre-pared to attack Issun Boshi, whereupon the hero leapt up and began attacking its eyes with his needle. Both oni soon fled, leaving behind them a mallet, an object of good luck. Issun Boshi and the girl struck the mallet on the ground and made a wish. Immediately, Issun Boshi grew into a full-size samurai. The couple returned home, and the girl's father agreed to allow them to be married.

ITCHITA, according to the Yakut people of Siberia, is an earth goddess and an aspect of the great mother goddess. She keeps sickness away from human beings, and is attended by the spirits of the grass and trees. She herself lives in the white beech tree. Other aspects of the great mother are the goddess Ynakhsyt, who protects cattle, and Ajysyt, who looks after children and helps women in childbirth. Ajysyt constantly sways backwards and forwards, thereby encouraging the growth of the life force.

IZANAGI AND IZANAMI

IZANAGI AND IZANAMI, according to Shinto belief, were the eighth pair of deities to appear after heaven and earth had been created out of chaos. Their full names, Izanagi-No-Mikoto and Izanami-No-Mikoto, mean "The August Male" and "The August Female".

Izanagi and Izanami were ordered to create the islands of Japan. They stood side by side on the "Floating Bridge of Heaven", lowered the heavenly jewelled spear into the sea and began to stir. When they lifted the spear out of the water, droplets fell from its tip and became an island, the first solid land. The two gods then descended on to the island and built a heavenly pillar and a splendid palace.

One day, the deities realized that each of their bodies differed from that of the other. Izanami said that her body was not fully formed in one place and Izanagi said that his body had been formed in excess in one place. Izanagi then suggested that they bring these two parts together. The two deities circled around the heavenly pillar until they met one another and joined their bodies together. Izanami bore a child, but he was a deformed creature called Hiruko, or "Leech Child", whom the couple immediately abandoned at sea. The gods decided that the child had been born imperfect as a result of Izanami having spoken first during the couple's courting ritual. Once again, the couple circled the pillar and this time, Izanagi spoke first.

Izanami subsequently gave birth to the islands of Japan as well as to the gods and goddesses of waterfalls, mountains, trees, plants and the wind. While giving birth to the god of fire, *KAGUTSUCHI*, Izanami was so badly burned that she died. However, even while dying she continued to bear more and more gods. Eventually, she disappeared to *YOMI*, the land of the dead.

Izanagi was desperately upset. Many deities were formed from his tears, and when he sliced off the fire god's head, even more deities came into being. Izanagi determined to follow his wife to Yomi, but by the time he arrived there she had already eaten the food of the dead. Although Izanami tried to persuade the gods to allow her to return to the land of the living, they refused her request. Izanagi then stormed into the hall of the dead and, after lighting a tooth of his comb and using it as a torch, he saw Izanami. She was horribly transformed: her corpse was squirming with maggots and eight thunder deities had taken up residence in her body.

Horrified at the sight of his wife, Izanagi fled back home. His behaviour infuriated Izanami, who sent the hags of Yomi, together with numerous thunder deities and warriors, to hunt him down. However, by employing various magic tricks, Izanagi succeeded in escaping them. When the god finally reached the outer edge of the land of the dead, he found three peaches. Picking them up, he threw them at the hags, who immediately ran away. Izanagi told the peaches that from that time onwards they would save mortals, just as they had saved him.

At length, Izanami, who by now had herself become a demon, set off in pursuit of Izanagi. In order to block her way, her husband pushed

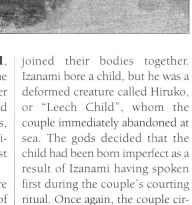
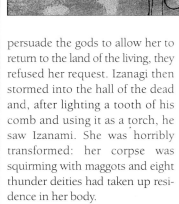

IZANAMI AND IZANAGI, standing on the "Floating Bridge of Heaven", stir the sea with the heavenly jewelled spear to create the world. (WOODBLOCK PRINT, 19TH CENTURY.)

a huge boulder into the passage that separated Yomi from the land of the living. The husband and wife stood on either side of the boulder, and Izanami told Izanagi that in punishment for his behaviour she would strangle a thousand people each day. Izanagi replied that, each day, he would ensure that 1,500 people were born.

The god then purified himself by washing in a river. When he removed his clothes, a new deity came into being as each garment fell to the ground. Finally, Izanagi washed his face and, in so doing, brought into existence the sun goddess *AMATERASU*, the moon god *TSUKIYOMI* and the storm god *SUSANO-WO*. Izanagi decided to divide his kingdom equally among these three deities. (See also *CREATION MYTHS*)

JAR-SUB, according to the ancient Turkic and modern Altaic peoples of Siberia, personifies the

which to rule his kingdom, he was bewitched by a god who took the form of a bear and caused the invaders to fall asleep. One of Jimmu-Tenno's followers dreamt of a magic sword sent by Amaterasu to help Jimmu-Tenno pacify the land now known as Yamato. When he awoke, the soldier found the sword and gave it to his leader. The forces continued on their journey, led by a crow. When they reached Yamato, Jimmu-Tenno built a magnificent palace and married a local princess.

JIZO-BOSATSU is the Japanese form of Kshitigarbha, the bodhisattva or "buddha-to-be" who protects children. He is also said to help pregnant women and travellers. His cult is extremely popular in Japan, where he tends to be regarded as a venerable person rather than as a deity. Each year, his devotees confess their faults to him in the ceremony known as the "Confession of Jizo".

According to one tale, dead children whose parents simply lament their deaths, rather than offering up prayers to help them to be reborn, are sent to a sandy beach or river bank in hell. There, they spend their time building shrines, which are destroyed each night by demons. However, Jizo eventually appears to console the children. He wraps them in the folds of his robe and tells them that he is their father and mother.

JIMMU-TENNO (below) was the legendary first emperor of Japan, from whom the Japanese Imperial family claims direct descent. (DRAWING, ANON. 20TH CENTURY.)

combination of earth and water. Jar-Sub can refer either to the universe as a whole, or to the native land.

JATA, according to a creation myth of the Dayak people of Borneo, was a divine maiden who made the land and the hills during the second epoch of creation. In the first epoch of creation, the clouds, the sky, the mountains, the cliffs, the sun and moon all came into being. Afterwards, the "Hawk of Heaven" and the great fish *ILA-ILAI LANGIT* were created, followed by two fabulous creatures, *DIDIS MAHENDERA* with the jewel eyes and *ROWANG RIWO* with the golden saliva. Finally, the golden headdress of the god *MAHATALA* appeared. In the third epoch of creation, the tree of life arose, thereby uniting the upper and lower worlds.

JIZO-BOSATSU (above) is sometimes represented as a monk. He carries a staff with rings whose jingling warns small creatures of his approach so he will not step on them. (CARVED WOOD, 11TH CENTURY.)

JIMMU-TENNO, according to Japanese mythology, was the first Emperor of Japan and thus the founder of the Imperial line. He was said to be the descendant of the sun goddess *AMATERASU* and the grandson of *HIKOHOHODEMI*. During his life, Jimmu-Tenno was known by two names, Toyo-Mike-Nu and Kamu-Yamato-Iware-Hiko; it was only after his death that he became known as Jimmu-Tenno. Jimmu-Tenno was said to have acceded to the throne in 660 BC.

One story tells how, while moving east with his troops in search of new territories and a place from

K

JUROJIN is one of the *SHICHI FUKUJIN* or seven gods of good fortune or happiness, an assembly of deities gathered together in the 17th century by a monk who intended them to symbolize the virtues of a man of his time.

Jurojin was the god of longevity and happy old age. He is depicted as a small old man with a long white beard and is shown in the company of a crane, tortoise or deer, all symbols of longevity. The god also carries a staff to which is attached a scroll or book, which is said to contain the wisdom of the world. He is said to be extremely fond of rice wine. (See also *THE SHICHI FUKUJIN*)

KADAKLAN, according to the mythology of the Tinguian people of Luzon in the Philippines, is the god of thunder. He lives in the sky and beats his drum to create thunder. His dog Kimat is the lightning; he bites whatever Kadaklan chooses.

KAGUTSUCHI, or Homosubi, is the fire god of Japanese Shinto mythology. He is the son of *IZANAMI*, the female half of the primal couple. When she gave birth to him, the goddess was so badly burned that she died. In revenge, *IZANAGI*, Kagutsuchi's father,

JUROJIN (left) is shown as a small old man with a long white beard. One of the Shichi Fukujin, or seven gods of good fortune or happiness, he holds the promise of happiness in old age. (IVORY NETSUKE.)

attacked the fire god, slicing off his head. In doing so, Izanagi created several more deities. Kagutsuchi was greatly feared by the Japanese.

KAMI was the word used in ancient Japan to refer to anything mysterious or sacred. Its range of application covered everything from objects of folk cults to important deities. The kami came to be regarded as supernatural beings with human qualities. Sometimes, they are nature deities such as mountains, trees and rivers; sometimes they embody values or ideals. They may be protective deities or important men. The Buddha was thought of as the kami of China, and, later on, local kami came to be regarded as protectors of Buddhism. Some became identified with Buddhist deities.

KAMI-MUSUBI see *OKUNINUSHI*.

KANNON see *KWANNON*.

THE KAPPA, according to Japanese mythology, are a race of monkey-like demons. They live in ponds and rivers, and lure human beings, as well as other creatures, down into the depths of the water where they then feed on them. As well as being particularly fond of blood, the kappa like cucumbers.

They are malicious creatures who can, however, sometimes be appeased or bargained with. For example, if a cucumber is inscribed with the names and ages of a particular family and thrown into the water where a kappa lives, the creature will not harm that family. The kappa also display a certain vulnerability. They always return a low bow, and in doing so they spill the water, which empowers them,

from the saucer-shaped depressions in the tops of their heads.

Because they are very knowing, they can sometimes prove helpful to human beings. According to one tale, a kappa persuaded a man on a horse to play tug-of-war with him. As soon as they had grasped hold of one another, the man spurred on his horse, and the water began to spill from the top of the kappa's head. The kappa begged the man to stop, promising that if he did so, he would teach him how to mend bones. The rider agreed, and his family became renowned for their knowledge of bone-setting.

The kappa have monkey-like faces, webbed hands and feet and yellow-green skin. They wear shells like tortoises.

KARITEI-MO see *KISHIMO-JIN*.

THE KAPPA (above) are demons who drag animals or people into rivers to feed on. They resemble monkeys but stink of fish. (ILLUSTRATION FROM MYTHS AND LEGENDS OF JAPAN.)

KHADAU see *MAMALDI*.

KHORI TUMED is a hero of Mongolian shamanism. One day, he saw nine swans fly on to the island of Oikhon on Lake Baikal. The swans removed their feathered garments and revealed themselves to be beautiful women. Believing that they were alone, they bathed naked in the lake. However, while the women were bathing, Khori Tumed stole one of their dresses and so, when they left the water, one of them was unable to fly away.

Khori Tumed married the swan woman and they lived happily together, eventually producing 11

sons. However, the time came when the swan woman asked Khori Tumed to give her back her feathers. The hero refused, but his wife continued to ask him for her dress, assuring him that she would not fly away. Eventually, Khori Tumed relented and allowed her to try the dress on. Immediately, she flew up and out of a window in their tent.

Before she finally escaped, Khori Tumed persuaded her to name their sons. The swan woman did so and then flew around the tent, bestowing blessings on the tribes.

KHOSADAM, according to the Yenisei people of Siberia, is the wife of *EC*, the supreme god. Ec drove her out of the sky after discovering that she had been unfaithful to him with the moon. Khosadam is an evil, destructive deity and appears as a devourer of souls.

KHUN K'AN see *THENS*.

KHUN K'ET see *THENS*.

KIMAT see *KADAKLAN*.

KISHIMO-JIN, or Karitei-Mo, is Japanese mythology's "Goddess Mother of Demons". She is said to eat children and to have destroyed a town in India while Gautama Buddha was living there. When the townspeople begged the Buddha to save them, he hid Kishimo-Jin's son beneath his begging bowl. The demoness was distraught and finally asked the Buddha for help. The Buddha converted her by explaining that the pain she felt at the loss of her son was similar to that she wilfully inflicted on other

KUNLUN, where Gautama Buddha sits enthroned, is regarded as a kind of earthly paradise by both Buddhists and Daoists.
(*BUDDHIST SCROLL.*)

KUNLUN, beyond the western limits of the ancient Chinese empire, was home to the "Queen Mother of the West".

people. Kishimo-Jin was thus converted to Buddhism and became a protector of children. She is often represented seated on a chair and holding a child in her arms.

KUAN-TI see *GUAN DI*.

KUAN YIN see *GUAN YIN*.

KUEI see *GUEI*
.

K'UN LUN see *KUNLUN*
.

KUNLUN, or K'un Lun, is a mountain range in western China that is regarded as a Daoist paradise. It is said to be the home of *XI WANG MU* and the immortals. As well as rising above the ground, it is said to descend underground, thereby connecting the realm of the dead with that of the gods. Xi Wang Mu, the "Queen Mother of the West" is said to grow the peaches of immortality in the garden of her splendid palace on Kunlun.

41

THE EIGHT IMMORTALS

DAOISM EMERGED AS A philosophical system at about the same time as Confucianism, around the sixth century BC. Later, in response to the growing popularity of Buddhism, it acquired all the trappings of a religion, including a mythology. The "Eight Immortals" were central figures in Daoist myth and Chinese folk religion. They had all gained eternal life through seeking the Daoist "Way", and each set an example of ideal behaviour that could be followed by ordinary people to gain enlightenment. Though they were not gods, their immortality gave them superhuman powers: they practised magic and could fly through the air at great speed. They had many adventures while pursuing their mission to banish evil from the world, and were all cheerfully addicted to wine, so that they were sometimes described as the Jiu-zhong Ba Xian – the "Eight Drunken Immortals".

LI TIEGUAI (far left, above) was the first immortal. His body was prematurely cremated while his soul was visiting a sacred mountain. As his own body was no longer available to him, his soul had to inhabit that of a lame beggar, and he used an iron crutch to support himself. Li later revived his disciple's dead mother with a phial of magic medicine, and came to be regarded as the patron of pharmacists. (RELIEF TILE, QING DYNASTY.)

HE XIANGU (second from right), the patron of unmarried girls, was a young woman herself who acquired immortality when a spirit appeared to her on the mountain where she lived and instructed her to grind and eat a mother-of-pearl stone. The stone made her weightless and able to fly over the mountains. She is usually shown carrying a peach or a lotus blossom. (RELIEF TILE, QING DYNASTY.)

CAO GUOJIU (far left) carried a golden tablet which allowed him admission to the imperial court, because he was the brother of the empress. He left the court to seek the Daoist "Way" but, when he found he had no money to pay a ferryman, he tried to impress him with his court credentials. The ferryman, who was Lu Dongbin in disguise, pointed out his folly, and Cao threw the tablet into the river. As an immortal, Cao Guojiu was the patron of the nobility. (RELIEF TILE, QING DYNASTY.)

SHOU LAO (left) the Daoist god of longevity, was visited by the "Eight Immortals" on one of their journeys together. Originally a stellar deity, the "Old Man of the South Pole", he had evolved into an old man who carried a gourd containing the water of life. He rode on a stag, a symbol of happiness. (CHINESE DISH, C. 1680.)

HAN XIANG (left), Lu Dongbin's disciple, was said to be the great-nephew of a Daoist philosopher. He was a wandering minstrel who played the flute. During the sea voyage of the "Eight Immortals", Ao Bing, son of the "Dragon King of the Eastern Sea", tried to steal the flute and take Han Xiang prisoner. There was a great battle to rescue Han Xiang, in which the immortals were, naturally, victorious. (IVORY FIGURE, MING DYNASTY.)

LU DONGBIN's (below) blessing on parents was believed to bestow intelligent children, so Chinese scholars regarded him especially highly, and he was the guardian of ink makers. When the "Eight Immortals" decided to cross the sea, they each threw down an object on which to ride, which each turned into a sea monster. Lu Dongbin used his magic sword. (LU DONGBIN RIDING ON A KRAKEN, FROM SUPERSTITIONS EN CHINE, 1915.)

LAN CAIHE (above) was either a girl or an effeminate man. She was the patron of the poor, because she gained her immortality by her kindness in attending to the needs of a filthy beggar, whose wounds she washed and dressed. The beggar turned out to be Li Tieguai, the first of the "Eight Immortals". Lan Caihe was sometimes shown with a basket of flowers, because of her skill in growing marvellous blooms from a small pot of earth. (FRESCO, QING DYNASTY.)

ZHANG GUOLAO (above) rode on a white mule, sometimes sitting facing the animal's tail. He was a great necromancer, and his mule had extraordinary powers. It could travel over vast distances but, when no longer required, it could be folded up like a sheet of paper and kept in a bag. Zhang Guolao is often depicted with the bag containing his mule, or hitting a bamboo drum. He granted both happy marriage and the gift of children. (IVORY AND BRONZE FIGURE, MING DYNASTY.)

ZHONG-LI QUAN (left) learnt the "Way" of Daoism from Li Tieguai, then disappeared into the clouds on achieving immortality and became the messenger of heaven. Bald, with a long beard, he carried a feather fan and was the patron of soldiers. Zhong-li Quan was sometimes also shown holding a peach. The peaches of Xi Wang Mu, the "Queen Mother of the West" ripened every 3,000 years, when the immortals ate them to renew their immortality. (IVORY FIGURE, MING DYNASTY.)

L

KWANNON, or Kannon, according to Japanese Buddhist belief, is the god or goddess of mercy. She is the Japanese form of the Chinese goddess *GUANYIN*, or Kuan Yin, who herself derives from the Indian male bodhisattva Avalokiteshvara. The feminization of Kwannon is relatively modern. Kwannon, as a bosatsu, or bodhisattva, is a "buddha-to-be" who has decided to remain on earth in order to help other people to achieve enlightenment. She is known as the "Lady Giver of Children" and is a very popular deity, the protector of women and children. Kwannon is said to have been born from a ray of light, which emerged from the right of the Buddha Amitabha. There is also a Kwannon with a horse's head and one with numerous arms. According to one

KWANNON (above) lived in a cave in the Iwai Valley. (WOODBLOCK PRINT BY HIROSHIGE, ANDO OR UTAGAWA, 1853.)

KWANNON (right), the Japanese god or goddess of mercy, could assume 33 different forms, including this one with 11 heads. (WOOD SCULPTURE, 12TH CENTURY.)

tradition, Kwannon could assume 33 different forms, which gave rise to a great ritual pilgrimage to 33 sanctuaries dedicated to her.

LAN CAIHE see *BA XIAN*.

LAO CHÜN see *LAO JUN*.

LAO JUN, or Lao Chün, is the name given to the deified form of Laozi, who, by tradition, wrote the Dao-de Jing, the text which forms the basis of Daoism. He is believed to have lived in the sixth century BC; his deification began in the second century BC. Lao Jun became one of the most important Daoist gods and was sometimes said to have arisen from the primordial chaos. According to another legend, he emerged from his mother's side after a gestation of 80 years.

LEI GONG, or Lei Kung, is the god of thunder in China's Daoist pantheon. Known as "My Lord Thunder", or "Thunder Duke", he is depicted as a horribly ugly man with wings, claws, and a blue body. He carries a drum, and in his hands he holds a mallet and a chisel. Lei Gong attacks any human being

guilty of an undetected crime or who remains beyond the reach of the earthly law.

One story tells how a fierce storm arose in the middle of a thick forest. A hunter looked up into the trees and saw a child holding a flag. Lei Gong, the thunder god, approached the child but as soon as the child waved the flag, he retreated. Immediately, the hunter realized that the child must be an evil spirit and that the flag must be made of some unclean material, since all deities dislike impure objects. The hunter shot down the flag, and Lei Gong instantly struck the tree in which the child was perched. Unfortunately, being so

LAO JUN (above) is said to have been a contemporary of Confucius and a teacher of the Buddha. (PAINTED SCROLL, 18TH CENTURY.)

LAO JUN (above right), who was reputed to have been born with white hair and the power of speech, lived to a very great age. (PAINTING BY QIAN GU, 16TH CENTURY.)

close to the tree, the hunter was also struck by the thunder. However, when he came round, the hunter found a message on his body saying that his life had been prolonged for 12 years in thanks for having assisted with the work of heaven. At the foot of the tree, the hunter found the body of a vast lizard, the real form of the child.

LEI GONG (above), the winged thunder god, harasses sheep and swine in a storm of thunder clouds and explosive lightning flashes. (WOODBLOCK PRINT, 19TH CENTURY.)

45

M

LEI KUNG see *LEI GONG*.

LI NAZHA see *NAZHA*.

LI TIEGUAI see *BA XIAN*.

THE LIGHTNING GODDESS is one of the nature deities referred to in early Chinese legends. She is the wife of the god of thunder, *LEI GONG*, and carries a pair of mirrors which she uses to create flashes of lightning and, occasionally, fires. The gods of thunder, lightning, wind and rain were invoked by the people during times of drought.

LING CHIH see *LING ZHI*.

LING ZHI, or Ling Chih, according to Daoist belief, is a plant of immortality. Its name means "magic herb". Ling zhi is believed to be either a type of grass or a mushroom. It grows on the three islands of the immortals, and anyone who eats it is said to gain immortality for at least 500 years.

LONG WANG, or Lung Wang, are "Dragon Kings" according to Chinese mythology. They are the servants either of Yuanshi Tian-Zong, the "Celestial Venerable of the Primordial Beginning", or *YU HUANG*, the "Jade Emperor", who was Yuanshi Tian-Zong's assistant and later came to surpass him in power. According to Daoist belief, there are different varieties of Long Wang: the celestial dragon kings, the dragon kings of the five cardinal points and the dragon kings of the oceans. Each of the dragon kings of the oceans has responsibility for one of the four oceans, helped by an army of sea creatures. The Long Wang bring rain.

LU DONGBIN see *BA XIAN*.

THE LIGHTNING GODDESS holding her two mirrors, which she flashes to cause lightning.

LUNG WANG see *LONG WANG*.

LUXING see *SAN XING*.

MAHATALA is the supreme god of the Dayak people of Borneo. He rules over the upper regions and lives on Jewel Mountain.

MAIDERE, according to the Altaic people of Siberia, was the saviour whom the great sky god *ULGAN* sent to earth in order to protect human beings from the evil ways of the god and first man *ERLIK*. Erlik succeeded in killing Maidere, whereupon the saviour's blood gave rise to vast flames, which leapt up to the skies, destroying Erlik's heaven.

MAIN is a mythical hero of the Evenk people of Siberia. One story tells how a great elk ran to the top of a hill in the upper world and impaled the sun on its antlers. Immediately, human beings, who lived in the middle world, were subjected to continual darkness. The hero Main flew to the upper world on a pair of skis and proceeded to hunt down the elk. He eventually succeeded in shooting

LONG WANG (above), a dragon king, holds court in this modern mural in a mountain temple in Shanxi province in northern China. It is said that the dragon kings live in their own crystal palaces beneath the water.

the animal with an arrow, whereupon sunshine returned to the middle world of human beings. Main remained in the upper world, guarding the sun. According to Evenk tradition, each evening the elk catches the sun and each night, Main pursues the elk and reclaims the sun in order to rise the next morning.

MAMALDI, according to the Amur people of Siberia, created the continent of Asia. She and her husband, Khadau, are regarded either as the first human couple or as the parents of the first shaman. Whereas Khadau created the souls

LONG WANG (left), a celestial dragon king. Because they were the bringers of rain, dragon kings controlled life and death.

of shamans, Mamaldi breathed life into them. She was eventually killed by Khadau.

MANUK MANUK, according to Sumatran mythology, is a fabulous blue chicken, which belonged to the supreme god. One day, the chicken laid three gigantic eggs from which emerged three gods. The gods created the three levels of the universe: the upper world, or heaven; the middle world, or the earth; and the underworld.

MARISHI-TEN is Japanese Buddhism's goddess, or sometimes god, of war and victory. In the Middle Ages, Japanese warriors believed that Marishi-Ten made them invisible. She is depicted either sitting or standing on a boar or herd of boars. She sometimes has as many as eight arms in which she holds numerous weapons.

LING ZHI (right), the fabled mushrooms of immortality, being gathered by a boy.
(DRAWING BY ZHANG LING, 16TH CENTURY.)

MEN SHEN consist of a pair of Chinese gods who look after entrances and doorways. One of the gods is usually represented with a red or black face, the other with a white one. They are armed with weapons and magic symbols, and guard houses as well as palaces. During the New Year festivities, paper images of the gods are stuck on doors to protect those that live within from evil demons.

Although their origins are supposed to lie in the ancient past – when they were said to prevent spirits escaping from hell – one pair of Men Shen was later said to represent two historical generals who heroically guarded the palace of a Tang dynasty emperor against demons. According to one myth, the emperor had promised to look after a dragon king who had made a mistake while distributing the rain and had been condemned to death by the "Jade Emperor", *YU HUANG*. However, the emperor was unable to keep his promise and the spirit of the dragon king held him responsible for his death. Each night, the dragon king would come and cause a commotion outside the palace gates. Unable to sleep, the emperor fell ill, so his two generals guarded the doors. Eventually, the dragon king was driven away.

MIROKU-BOSATSU is the Japanese form of Maitreya, the future buddha. He currently lives in the Tushita heaven awaiting his future birth as a human being and finally as a buddha.

MOMOTARO is a Japanese hero who was born from a peach and was renowned for conquering demons. An elderly couple, who had been unable to have children, found a peach floating in a stream. When they cut the fruit open, they found a tiny baby boy inside. The baby sat up and ate the peach, whereupon the delighted couple called him Momotaro or "Peach Child". They raised Momotaro to be a brave and noble boy.

When he was 15, he decided to repay his parents and friends for looking after him, and determined to rid a neighbouring island of the *ONI*, or devils, which were persecuting them. Momotaro pocketed three dumplings, which the old woman had cooked, and set off for the island. He soon encountered a dog, a pheasant and a monkey, each of whom agreed to accompany him on his quest in return for a dumpling. The four adventurers then took a boat and crossed over to the island. There, they found

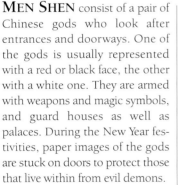

MEN SHEN (above left), one of a pair of entrance gods, guards a Chinese temple door in Yogjakarta, Java.

MEN SHEN (above), guarding a temple entrance, are sometimes represented as two generals, Heng and Ha, whose weapons include poisonous breath and fire.

numerous girls who had been taken prisoner by the oni. Momotaro attacked the castle of the oni and, together with his companions, succeeded in killing all the devils. He then piled his boat high with the treasure that the oni had stolen from the village people, helped the captive girls on board and returned home a hero.

MONJU-BOSATSU is the Japanese form of the bodhisattva, or "buddha-to-be", Manjushri. His name means "he whose beauty

MOMOTARO (left), before his battle with the oni, enlisted the help of a pheasant in exchange for a dumpling . (ILLUSTRATION FROM MYTHS AND LEGENDS OF JAPAN.)

MOYANG KAPIR is a civilizing hero spirit, according to the Ma'Betisek people of Malaysia. He stole the bag that contained the rules of civilized human behaviour from the ferocious spirit *MOYANG MELUR* and then distributed them among his people in order that they might no longer commit murder, cannibalism and incest.

MOYANG MELUR, according to the Ma'Betisek people of Malaysia, is a spirit being who guarded the rules of civilized behaviour. He is said to live on the moon and to be half-human, half-tiger. For a long time, Moyang

charms", and he personifies wisdom, compassion and contemplation. Monju-Bosatsu is often shown accompanied by a lion and is usually seated, holding the sword of intelligence, which cuts through ignorance.

Melur kept the rules of civilized behaviour to himself and, as a result, human beings constantly committed murder, incest and cannibalism.

One night, Moyang Melur was so enthralled by the chaos and destruction that was taking place below him that he leaned right out of the moon in order to take a closer look. However, he leaned too far and fell to earth. There, he met a hunter called *MOYANG KAPIR*. Moyang Melur told Moyang Kapir that unless he was able to return to

MIROKU (left), the future buddha, sits in contemplation, awaiting the time of his coming on earth. (JAPANESE SCULPTURE.)

MONJU-BOSATSU (above right), the Japanese form of Manjushri, with the Buddha (seated in the centre) and the bodhisattva Fugen-Bosatsu. (14TH CENTURY.)

the moon immediately, he would kill every single human being. Moyang Kapir promptly threw a rope to the moon, and they both climbed up it.

Moyang Melur was looking forward to killing and eating Moyang Kapir, but the latter quickly slid back down to earth, taking with him the rules of civilized behaviour, which he had found hidden in a bag under a mat. The hunter then distributed the rules among his people.

SHAMANS OF MONGOLIA

IN MANY TRADITIONAL COMMUNITIES, the shaman is a central figure combining the function of priest and doctor. He or she has the power to control spirits which, though neither good nor evil, may be destructive: to protect the community he or she incorporates them in him or herself. The shaman's ability to make out-of-body journeys to the upper and lower spirit worlds is also part of a protective role in the tribe. In shamanistic myths the world was once peopled by beings who could easily travel between heaven and earth, but after the bridge between the two was broken, most people lost their original wisdom. Eventually only a few – the shamans – were able to reach heaven, and they could do so only in spirit, by separating their souls from their bodies. Shamanistic myths, passed down through successive generations in an oral tradition, tell of a process of decline, from a golden age, when great spirits brought knowledge to the world, to the present, when not even all shamans can fly away from it.

DRUMMING (above) is used to induce a trance state in which the shaman's soul can leave his body. The drum beat excludes other stimuli while its insistent rhythm works on the consciousness. According to Mongolian legend, early shamans could use their drums to call back the souls of the dead. The lord of the dead, fearing that he would lose all his subjects, ordained that the shamans' drums, originally double-headed, should have only a single head to reduce their power.

ANIMALS (left) are used by Siberian Yakut shamans as receptacles for their souls. Each shaman keeps his chosen animal far away from other people, so that its life is protected and his spiritual well-being ensured. However, once a year, when the last snow melts, the animals are said to come down from the mountains and walk into the villages. The most powerful shamans keep their souls in horses, elks, bears, eagles or boars; the weakest keep them in dogs. Sometimes the animals fight, and if one is harmed, its shaman will fall ill or die.

YAKUT SHAMANS *(above) claim descent from a primordial shaman who rebelled against the supreme god and was condemned to eternal fire. His body, which was composed of reptiles, was consumed, but a single frog escaped the flames and gave rise to a line of shamanic demons from whom Yakut shamans are still drawn. (*LITHOGRAPH, C. 1835.*)*

A SHAMAN *(left) enacts a healing ceremony over a sick man. Illness is thought to be due to the loss of the person's soul, which may have wandered to the land of the dead in error, looking for its home. The shaman's task is to retrieve the soul and for this he or she needs to be able to fly to the underworld and persuade it to return. The shaman may also massage, stroke or blow on the patient, and suck harmful material out through the skin. (*A SHAMAN OF YAKUTIA, C. 1805.*)*

N

MUCILINDA's (left) multiple heads, with their cobra-like hoods, spread out like an umbrella to shelter the seated Buddha, here represented by an empty seat. (STONE CARVING.)

MUCILINDA (left) coiled his body under the Buddha beneath the sacred fig tree at Bodhi-gaya (STONE CARVING, 3RD CENTURY AD.)

MUCILINDA is the king of the serpent deities, or water spirits, known as *NAGAS*. According to a legend, Mucilinda sheltered the Buddha with the outspread hoods of his seven heads during a downpour that lasted for seven days. When the sun returned, the serpent was transformed into a young prince who proceeded to pay homage to the Buddha. In India, and especially in South-east Asia, Mucilinda is often depicted protecting the Buddha.

NAGA PADOHA is the great sea serpent of South-east Asian mythology. In the tale of creation, *BATARA GURU*, a form of the great Hindu god Shiva, created the first solid land whereupon Naga Padoha sought to destroy it by writhing and thrashing about in the ocean. However, Batara Guru, in his incarnation as a hero figure, managed to control the serpent, pressing him down with a vast iron weight so that he descended to the lower regions of the cosmos.

NAGAS, according to the mythology of South-east Asia, are supernatural beings who take the form of serpents. The great serpent Sesha, on whose coils the god Vishnu rested in the intervals between creation, was served by nagas. In Buddhist belief, the serpent *MUCILINDA* was a naga king who sheltered Gautama Buddha from the weather. In Tibetan Buddhism, the nagas are said to guard the Buddhist scriptures. (See also *DEMONS*)

NAZHA, the "Third Prince" and *enfant terrible* of Chinese mythology, is an exorcising spirit and a deity of popular religion. Nazha is also said to have been a powerful deity in his own right, dispatched down to the human world by *YU HUANG*, the "Jade Emperor", to subdue or destroy the demons raging through the world. He was incarnated as the third son of Li Jing, a general who fought for the Zhou dynasty in the 12th century BC. Nazha grew up to be full of mischief and the numerous legends surrounding his life are probably better known to Chinese peasants than recent imperial history.

NGA, according to the mythology of the Samoyed Yuraks of Siberia, is the god of death and hell, and one of the two great demiurges, or supreme deities. One tale relates how the earth threatened to collapse, so a shaman visited *NUM*, the other great demiurge, and asked him for advice. Num instructed the shaman to descend below the earth and call upon Nga. The shaman did so and married Nga's daughter. He then supported the earth in his hand and became known as the "Old Man of the Earth".

NINIGI, or Honinigi, is the grandson of the great *AMATERASU*, the sun goddess of Japanese Shinto

NAGAS (below) are spirits in the form of serpents. They may be benevolent and protective, like Mucilinda sheltering the Buddha from the rain. (THAI BRONZE, 1291.)

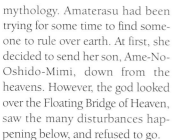

mythology. Amaterasu had been trying for some time to find someone to rule over earth. At first, she decided to send her son, Ame-No-Oshido-Mimi, down from the heavens. However, the god looked over the Floating Bridge of Heaven, saw the many disturbances happening below, and refused to go.

The gods all met together in order to decide what to do and eventually determined to send down Ame-No-Hohi. Three years passed but the gods heard nothing from Ame-No-Hohi. They then decided to send down his son, Ame-No-Wakahiko. Before he left, they gave him a bow and arrows.

Ame-No-Wakahiko descended to earth and soon married Shitateru-Hime, the daughter of *OKUNINUSHI*, the god of medicine and magic. This time, eight years passed without the gods hearing any news. At the end of that time, they sent down a pheasant to find out what Ame-No-Wakahiko had

NAZHA (above), the "Third Prince" and son of Li Jing, is the enfant terrible of Chinese mythology. Numerous popular legends are told about his escapades.

been doing. The pheasant perched on a tree outside the god's house.

One of the women of the house noticed the bird and told Ame-No-Wakahiko that it was an evil omen. Immediately, the god shot it with his bow and arrow. The arrow passed straight through the bird, entered heaven and fell at the feet of Amaterasu and the god Takami-Masubi. The god recognized the arrow and, in fury, flung it back down to earth where it killed Ame-No-Wakahiko. Shitateru-Hime, his wife, was devastated.

The gods then sent two of their number down to visit Okuninushi. They told him that they had been sent by the sun goddess in order to bring the land under her command. Okuninushi spoke to his two sons. The older son agreed to

worship Amaterasu, but the younger son tried to resist. However, the two gods soon overpowered the younger son, who then promised not to put up any resistance against the sun goddess. Okuninushi also agreed to the sun goddess's rule, on condition that a place should be reserved for him among the major deities worshipped at the famous shrine at Izumo. Amaterasu agreed to this.

At last, Amaterasu sent her grandson, Ninigi, down to earth. Before leaving heaven, Ninigi was given various divine objects, including the mirror into which the sun goddess had gazed after emerging from hiding in the cave, the heavenly jewels that had produced Amaterasu's sons and the sword Kusanagi, which the storm god *SUSANO-WO* had found in the tail of the eight-headed snake, Yamato-No-Orochi. These three items became the emblems of Japanese imperial power.

NAZHA's (above) father, Li Jing, was a commander who fought during the mythological wars between dynasties in the 12th century BC.

Ninigi married Kono-Hana-Sakuyu-Hime, the daughter of a mountain god. When Kono-Hana-Sakuyu-Hime conceived on the first night that she slept with her husband, Ninigi suspected her of having been unfaithful to him. In response, Kono-Hana-Sakuyu-Hime built a house with no doors, and, when she was about to give birth, she entered the house and set it alight saying that if she had been unfaithful, her child would die. As it turned out, Kono-Hana-Sakuyu-Hime produced three sons. One of them, *HIKOHOHODEMI*, married the daughter of the sea god. Their child later fathered a boy who, after his death, became known as *JIMMU-TENNO*. Jimmu-Tenno was the founder of the imperial line of Japan.

O

THE NIO, according to Japanese Buddhism, are the two guardian kings, or kings of compassion. They are usually represented as giants who guard the entrances to temples and monasteries, and are dressed either in sarongs or in armour. They are believed to banish evil spirits and thieves, and to protect children.

NU GUA or Nü Kua, is an ancient Chinese creator deity who, after the great flood, became the consort of *FU XI*. Her name is derived from the words for gourd or melon, a symbol of fertility, and she is sometimes known as the "Gourd Girl". Nu Gua is said to have been half-human and half-serpent or dragon and to have had the ability to change her shape at will. She is sometimes shown holding a pair of compasses while Fu Xi holds a set square, symbolizing their part in the creation. Nu Gua is also said to have invented the flute.

According to one story, Nu Gua descended to earth after it had been separated from the sky, and after the mountains, rivers, animals and plants had been created. She tamed the wild animals and, together with other mythological figures, taught humankind how to irrigate the land. However, Nu Gua is most famous for having created human beings out of clay or mud.

One day, as Nu Gua wandered through the world, she began to feel that something was missing and longed to have some companionship. She sat down on the bank of a river and, gazing at her reflection in the water, she began to play with some mud from the riverbed. Almost without thinking, she began to model the clay into a little figure. However, rather than giving the figure a tail like herself, she gave it legs and feet. When Nu Gua had finished moulding the figure, she stood it on the ground and it immediately came to life, dancing and laughing with happiness.

Nu Gua was so happy with her creation that she decided to fill the whole world with people. She worked until it grew dark, and as soon as the sun rose the next morning, she set to work once more. Although the people wandered off, Nu Gua could still hear their voices and so she never again felt lonely. Before long, Nu Gua realized that she could not possibly create enough people to populate the whole earth. She decided to call on her magic power and, taking a length of vine, she trailed it in the mud and then whirled it about in the air. As soon as the drops of mud touched the ground, they were transformed into human beings.

It is sometimes said that those people whom Nu Gua fashioned with her hands became rich and fortunate, whereas those who were created when the drops of mud fell to the ground were the poor and humble people.

NU GUA's (left) image on a Chinese temple altar in Singapore. She is known as the "Dark Lady of the Ninth Heaven".

THE NIO (left) are the two guardian kings or kings of compassion. They are usually represented as temple guardians, with fierce expressions which are designed to deter evil spirits from entering the sacred precinct.

Realizing that her little people might eventually die and become extinct, Nu Gua divided them into male and female so that they could bear children.

Nu Gua and Fu Xi are also renowned for having saved the world from a flood. One tale tells how the world had become wild and chaotic: human beings were eaten by wild animals, immense fires raged continuously and water flowed without ceasing. Nu Gua mended the skies with melted stones, supported the heavens with the legs of a turtle and piled ashes of reeds on a river bank to dam the waters until, at last, everything became calm again.

NÜ KUA see *NU GUA*.

NUM and *NGA*, according to the mythology of the Samoyed Yuraks of Siberia, are the two great demiurges, or supreme deities. At the beginning of time, Num sent several birds one after the other to explore the endless stretches of water. Eventually, one of the birds returned with a small piece of sand or mud, from which Num created a floating island.

Another tale relates how the earth threatened to collapse, whereupon a shaman visited Num and asked him for advice. Num instructed the shaman to descend to Nga, the god of death and hell, who lived beneath the earth. The shaman did as instructed and married the daughter of Nga. He then supported the earth in his hand and became known as the "Old Man of the Earth". Num lives in a place of light, but he regularly visits earth to ensure it is secure.

OGETSU-NO-HIME see *UKE-MOCHI*.

大国主命さまは恋愛良縁の守り神と
して有名です。因幡の白兎を助けられた
心のやさしい神さまでみんなに幸福を与えて下さいます。

ご利益

京都 地主神社

良縁祈願

恋愛 結婚

京都 地主神社

OKUNINUSHI, according to Japanese Shinto mythology, is the god of medicine and magic. His name means "Great Land Master", and he ruled the earth after its creation until *AMATERASU* sent her grandson *NINIGI* to take his place. As god of medicine, he is credited with having invented therapeutic methods of healing.

Okuninushi had 80 brothers, all of whom wanted to marry the beautiful princess *YAKAMI* or Ya-Gami-Hime. While the brothers were on their way to visit the princess, a flayed hare stopped them and asked them for help. The brothers told the hare to wash in the sea and then dry itself in the wind. The hare suffered excruciating pain and distress. The creature then met Okuninushi who, feeling sorry for it, told it to bathe in fresh water and then roll around in the pollen of kama grass. The hare did as Okuninushi advised and imme-

diately felt better. In gratitude, the hare, who was really a god, told Okuninushi that the beautiful princess Yakami would be his.

Okuninushi's brothers were furious. They heated a vast rock until it was white-hot and rolled it down a mountain towards their brother. Okuninushi mistook the rock for a boar, caught hold of it and was burned to death. However, with the help of his mother, Kami-Musubi, he was brought back to life. The brothers then crushed Okuninushi to death. This time, Kami-Musubi advised her son to avoid further attacks by taking refuge in the underworld.

There, Okuninushi met the storm god *SUSANO-WO* and his daughter Suseri-Hime. The couple fell in love. When Susano-Wo discovered this, he sent Okuninushi to sleep in a room full of snakes. However, the god was protected by a scarf, which Suseri-Hime had

given him. The following night, Susano-Wo sent him to sleep in a room full of centipedes and wasps, but again Okuninushi was protected. Susano-Wo then fired an arrow into the middle of an enormous field and told Okuninushi to look for it. When Okuninushi reached the middle of the field, Susano-Wo set fire to the grass. However, a mouse showed Okuninushi a hole in which he could take shelter from the fire and then brought the arrow to him.

By this time, Susano-Wo was beginning to approve of Okuninushi. He asked him to wash his hair and then went to sleep. While Susano-Wo was sleeping, Okuninushi tied the storm god's hair to the rafters of his palace and fled with Suseri-Hime. He took with him Susano-Wo's sword, bow and arrows and his harp, called Koto. As Okuninushi and Suseri-Hime made their escape, the harp

OKUNINUSHI is seen here with the white hare of Inaoa, who foretold his success in his quest for the hand of Yakami.

brushed against a tree, and the noise of its strings awoke Susano-Wo. The god jumped up and in so doing pulled down his house with his hair.

Okuninushi hurried onwards. Eventually, at the borders of the underworld, Susano-Wo almost caught up with the elopers and called out to them, advising Okuninushi to fight his brothers with Susano-Wo's weapons in order that he might rule the world. It seems that Okuninushi's trickery had finally convinced the storm god that he would make a suitable husband for Suseri-Hime, because he then asked the god to make Suseri-Hime his wife and to build a palace at the foot of Mount Uka. Okuninushi became ruler of the province of Izumo.

P

OTSHIRVANI, according to Siberian mythology, is a god of light. He was sent by the supreme god to fight Losy, a monstrous serpent who killed all mortal beings by covering the world with poison. Otshirvani took the form of an enormous bird and, seizing Losy in his claws, threw him against the world mountain, killing him.

PA HSIEN see *BA XIAN*.

PAMALAK BAGOBO, according to the Bagobo people of Mindanao in the Philippines, is the god who created human beings. According to tradition, monkeys once behaved and looked like humans and only acquired their current appearance when Pamalak decided to create humankind as a separate race.

P'AN-KU see *PANGU*.

PANGU, or P'an-ku, is the cosmic giant of Chinese mythology. He is said to be the child of *YIN* and

THE ONI are giant horned demons. They are said to have come to Japan from China with the arrival of Buddhism, and Buddhist priests perform annual rites in order to expel them. The oni can be a variety of colours and have three fingers, three toes and sometimes three eyes. They are usually cruel and lecherous, and they are said to sweep down from the sky in order to steal the souls of people who are about to die. One story tells how the diminutive hero *MOMOTARO* freed numerous young girls whom the oni had captured and raped.

The oni of hell have the heads of oxen or horses; they hunt down sinners and take them away in their chariot of fire to *EMMA-O*, the ruler of the underworld. Some oni are held responsible for illness and disease, and others are said to have once been mortal women whose jealousy or grief transformed them into demons.

OT, the fire queen of the Mongols, is said to have been born at the beginning of the world, when the earth and sky separated. Her blessing is invoked at weddings and her radiance is said to penetrate throughout all the realms. Ot is believed originally to have been identical with *UMAI*, mother goddess of the Turkic people of Siberia.

PANGU is the giant who emerged from the cosmic egg when it split to form the earth and sky. He held the two apart to create the world.

PANGU, *the cosmic creator and mythological deity, on an altar in a temple in Tainan, in southern Taiwan.*

the myth tells how Pangu was born from the five basic elements and formed heaven and earth with a chisel and hammer. Pangu is still worshipped by some of the people of South China. (See also *CREATION MYTHS; CHINA'S SACRED PEAKS*)

PENG LAI, or P'eng-lai, according to Daoist belief, is an island in the East China Sea inhabited by the immortals or *XIAN*. The plant of immortality, *LING ZHI,* grows there. Many explorers have attempted to discover the mythical island, but all expeditions have failed – sometimes, it is said, because the island sinks beneath the waves. Everything on the miraculous island is made of gold and jewels: the trees are made of pearl and coral, and the animals and birds are glittering white.

The two other islands of the immortals are Fangchang and Yingzhou. Originally, there were five islands, but a giant caused two of them to break away from their moorings and sink without trace. Fangchang, lying off the east coast of China, is said to be inhabited by dragons and to boast marvellous palaces made of gold, jade and crystal. Thousands of immortals live there, cultivating the plant of immortality. Yingzhou is also credited with a marvellous appearance and inhabitants.

P'ENG-LAI see *PENG LAI.*

POLONG, according to Malayan and Indonesian tradition, is a flying demon created from the blood of a murdered man. Whoever owns the Polong can order it to attack his enemies. The victims tear their clothes, go blind and eventually lose consciousness. However, the Polong also feeds on the blood of its owner.

PU LANG SEUNG see *THENS.*

YANG, the vital forces of the universe. The myth of Pangu's birth tells how, at the very beginning of time, only chaos existed. Chaos took the form of a primordial egg, and eventually Pangu took shape inside its shell. The creature slept and grew inside the egg for 18,000 years until, eventually, he woke up and stretched. The light part of the egg, which was pervaded by yang, rose up to become the sky; the heavy part, pervaded by yin, sank down and became the earth.

Pangu, fearing that the earth and sky might merge together again, stood between them, his head keeping the sky aloft and his feet treading down the earth. For 18,000 years, the distance between heaven and earth increased at a rate of 3 metres (ten feet) a day. Pangu grew at the same rate to continue to hold heaven and earth apart.

Eventually, when Pangu considered that there was no risk of the earth and sky rejoining, he fell asleep and eventually died. The giant's enormous corpse gave rise to all the elements. His breath became the wind and clouds, his voice became the thunder and lightning, his left eye became the sun, and his right eye became the moon. His four limbs and his trunk were transformed into the cardinal directions and the mountains, his blood became the rivers and his veins the roads. His flesh became trees and soil, the hair on his head and his beard became the stars in the sky, and the hairs on his body were transformed into grass and flowers. His teeth and bones became metal and stones, and his sweat produced the dew. Finally, the fleas and parasites on his body became the ancestors of the different races of human beings.

Many later tales elaborate the story of Pangu. According to one, the alternation of night and day occurs when Pangu opens and closes his eyes. Another version of

CHINESE DRAGONS

THE CHINESE DRAGON CAME FIRST in the mythical hierarchy of 360 scaly creatures, and was one of the four animals who symbolized the cardinal points. Associated with the east, the dragon stood for sunrise, spring and fertility and was opposed by the white tiger of the west, who represented death. Daoist dragons were benevolent spirits associated with happiness and prosperity, and were kind to humans. However, when Buddhism became popular, their character was modified by the Indian concept of the naga, which was a more menacing creature. In folk religion, the Long Wang

were dragon kings who had authority over life and death because they were responsible for rain, without which life could not continue, and funerals. They were gods of rivers, lakes and oceans, and represented wisdom, strength and goodness. Because they had power over the rain, offerings were made to dragons during droughts, but angry Long Wang sent storms, fog and earthquakes. They protected ferrymen and water-carriers, and punished anyone who wasted water.

THE CHINESE DRAGON (above) was a mythical hybrid monster with the "horns of a deer, head of a camel, abdomen of a cockle, scales of a carp, claws of an eagle, feet of a tiger, and ears of an ox." Because dragons represented the yang principle, their images were traditionally accompanied by water or clouds, which were yin. (QIANLONG, FAMILLE ROSE BOTTLE VASE, 18TH CENTURY.)

DRAGON PROCESSIONS (left), which were held all over China in spring, welcomed the annual return of these generous creatures and ensured fertility. Dragons spent the winter underground, emerging on the second day of the second lunar month. Their arrival, announced by claps of thunder, coincided with the beginning of the spring rains, and this was the time to go out into the fields and begin the year's cultivation. As bringers of rain, dragons were coloured blue-green. (HSTE YANG, PROCESSION OF THE BLUE DRAGON.)

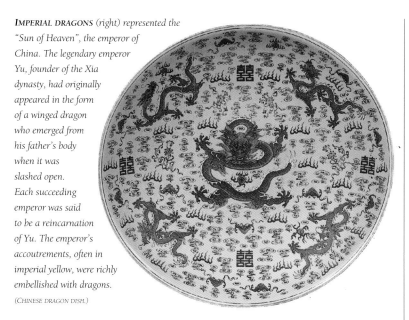

IMPERIAL DRAGONS (right) represented the "Sun of Heaven", the emperor of China. The legendary emperor Yu, founder of the Xia dynasty, had originally appeared in the form of a winged dragon who emerged from his father's body when it was slashed open. Each succeeding emperor was said to be a reincarnation of Yu. The emperor's accoutrements, often in imperial yellow, were richly embellished with dragons. (CHINESE DRAGON DISH.)

A DRAGON (above) was often depicted playing with a flaming pearl or ball, which symbolized thunder. It was this heavenly sport which was thought to cause the rain to fall. Only imperial dragons were represented with five claws on each foot. Those with four claws signified the status of a prince, while court officials were allowed only three claws for the dragons embroidered on their robes and other possessions. (CHINESE PILLAR RUG.)

HUI-NENG (right), the Chinese Buddhist patriarch, persuaded a fierce dragon to shrink so small that it would fit into a tiny rice bowl and was thus able to subdue it. The magic powers of dragons included the ability to make themselves invisible at will and change their shape and size. They could shrink to the size of a silkworm or swell to fill all the space between heaven and earth. (ILLUSTRATION FROM SUPERSTITIONS EN CHINE, 1914.)

R

PUDAI (left), in the "Cave of the Laughing Buddha" in Zhejiang Province, China, is portrayed with a fat belly and a wide grin.

PUDAI (right), also known as the "Hempbag Monk", on a temple altar in Tainan, in southern Taiwan.

PU-TAI see *PUDAI*.

PUDAI, or Pu-tai, was a Chinese monk who is said to have lived in the tenth century AD and whose original name was Qizi. He is said to have earned his name, which means "Hempen Sack", from his habit of wandering through towns with a beggar's sack on his back. He was believed to be able to predict the weather, and his life was filled with miraculous events. At his death, he revealed himself to be an incarnation of Maitreya, the future Buddha. Pudai is often represented as the "Laughing Buddha", the Chinese style of depicting Maitreya.

PULANG GANA, according to the Iban people of Borneo, is an earth spirit who ensures the abundant growth of rice. According to tradition, a long time ago the Iban began to clear the jungle in order to create the first rice farm. However, when they arose the next morning, they found that all the trees had grown back. The same happened after their next attempt to clear the jungle, and the next. At last, the Iban decided to keep watch during the night in order to try and solve the mystery.

That night, they saw Pulang Gana coax the trees back to life and ensure that they became rooted in the soil once more. They tried to catch the spirit, who explained that he owned the earth and everything that grew in it, and that he alone could ensure that the plants flourished. When the people asked the spirit what they should do before cultivating rice, he told them that they should offer up gifts to him.

QORMUSTA, or Chormusta, according to Mongolian belief, is king of the Tengri, the realms of

heaven. The supreme god, he lives in the centre of the world and is associated with the creation of fire.

RADIN is a mythical hero of the Iban people of Borneo. One tale tells how, after winning a battle, Radin began to be troubled by a hungry ghost. When the ghost introduced smallpox to Radin's tribe, the hero determined to kill it. One night, Radin hid inside a roll of matting, and when the ghost approached, he jumped out and cut it into pieces with his sword. Before falling asleep again, Radin heard something fall to the ground and, when daylight came, he found a carving of a hornbill, a sacred bird, lying on the ground in pieces. Radin realized that this signified that the ghost was far too powerful a being to overcome, so he and his people moved to another area.

THE RAIN SPIRIT is one of the early nature gods who were referred to in Chinese legendary stories. In his struggle with *HUANG DI*, the "Yellow Emperor", *CHIYOU* begged

THE RAIN SPIRIT (left), with his vase of water, sometimes also holds a dragon on a plate, since the dragon is a symbol of rain.

RANGDA (right), the Balinese demon queen, is represented by a terrifying mask.

the "Wind God" and the "Master of Rain" to bring on a major storm, with gales and torrential rains to help him. Along with the *LIGHT-NING GODDESS* and the God of Thunder, these nature spirits were invoked during times of drought. The Goddess of Lightning flashes the two mirrors she carries to cause lightning, while thunder is made by the thunder god with his hammer and drums, and has the power to kill. The Master of Rain is said to own a mysterious one-legged bird, which can drink the seas dry.

RANGDA is the terrifying demon queen of Bali. She leads an army of evil witches against *BARONG*, the leader of the forces of good. The evil demon is usually represented as scantily clad, with long hair and with claws in place of fingernails and toenails.

It is sometimes suggested that Rangda derived from an 11th-century Balinese queen who was exiled

by the king for practising witchcraft against his second wife. In revenge, Rangda attempted to destroy the kingdom. Half the population died of plague before she was overcome by the superior powers of a holy man. The name Rangda means "widow". (See also *DEMONS*)

ROWANG RIWO is a fabulous creature who, according to the Dayak people of Borneo, appeared during the first epoch of creation with *DIDIS MAHENDERA*. Rowang Riwo had golden saliva and Didis Mahendera had eyes of jewels.

THE SAN QING DAOZU's senior deity is Yuanshi Tian-zong, "Jade Pure", who is invisible and eternal.

THE SAN GUAN DADI, or San Kuan Ta-ti, are the "Three Great Primordial Rulers" and "Controllers of Heaven, Earth and the Waters". Also known as the San Yuan Dadi, they are of mythical origin and are revered as the source of all happiness and forgiveness of sins, able to avert calamities and sickness. Legend has it that *YU HUANG*, the "Jade Emperor", sent them down to earth to govern it, and observe men's good and evil thoughts and deeds.

SAN-HSING see *SAN XING*.

THE SAN QING DAOZU's second deity is Ling-bao Tian-zong, who regulates time and yin and yang.

SAN KUAN TA-TI see *SAN GUAN DADI*.

THE SAN QING DAOZU, or, as they are sometimes known, "The Three Pure Ones", are the supreme deities of the orthodox Daoist pantheon, ruling the entire cosmos from the highest heaven. In the "Doctrine of the Three Pure Ones", they are the symbolic personification of the three life principles: breath, vital essence and spirit. They are prayed to as a group for assistance in coping with the problems of life.

THE SAN QING DAOZU's third deity is Lao Jun. He is the deified form of the legendary founder of Daoism, Laozi.

SAN GUAN DADI, the three great primordial rulers, are transcendent powers who bestow happiness, forgive sins and protect from evil.

The first is the "Perfect One", or "Jade Pure", Yuanshi Tian-zong, the deity of the beginning representing primeval origins. He is in charge of the "Heaven of the Heavenly Ones" and is said to have formulated the heavens and earth and dominated the first phase of creation.

The "Highest Holy One", Ling-bao Tian-zong, the "High Pure", represents energy and activity. He is in charge of the "Heaven of the Perfect Ones", Zhenren, and is said to have devised the rules for calculating time and controlling the interaction of *YIN* and *YANG*, as well as the doctrine for the heavens and earth. He is the guardian of magical writings. Ling-bao dominated the second phase of creation.

The "Greatest Holy One", the "Supreme Pure", *LAO JUN*, representing humankind, is the deified philosopher Laozi who is in charge of the third and lowest heaven, that of the immortals. He is said to have dominated the third phase of the creation of the cosmos, and inspired the formation of religious Daoism at a later stage.

THE SAN XING, or San-hsing, or "Three Stars", are the three Chinese gods of good fortune. They were historical figures who were given divine status in recognition of their special merits. Fuxing or "Lucky Star" is usually depicted alongside a child or as a bat, a symbol of good luck. He is the god of happiness. Luxing or "Star of Honour" is the god of salaries and is often shown as a deer. Shouxing, "Star of Longevity", is shown with the face of an old man, a white beard and eyebrows, a high bald head and holding a knotty staff, a symbol of the immortals.

Fuxing is said to have been a government official called Yang Cheng who lived during the sixth century BC. He came from a village whose inhabitants were all very short in height. Each year, the emperor, who enjoyed surrounding himself with dwarfs, would call a number of the villagers to his court and insist that they remain there. As a result, as time went by, the

THE SAN XING (left) are the most important spirits of the stars of the constellation Ursa Minor. (CHINESE PORCELAIN DISH, 18TH CENTURY.)

population of the village began to dwindle. Eventually, Yang Cheng asked the emperor to take pity on the village folk. The emperor was impressed by Yang Cheng's petition and so ceased his demands.

Luxing is also identified with Guo Ziyi, who had many sons, or is said to have been Shi Fei, a servant of the founder of the Han dynasty, who lived at the end of the third century BC.

Shouxing came to be known as *SHOU LAO*, the god of long life and "Old Man of the South Pole". He is said to fix the date of everyone's death, writing it down beforehand. However, although the digits of the appointed date cannot be changed, they can sometimes be juggled.

According to one tale, a child called Zao Yan was told that he had only 19 more years to live. One day, the boy was told to go to a field, taking with him some food and wine. There, he would find two men playing a game of draughts (checkers) under a mulberry tree. Zao Yan was advised to offer the men food and drink but to refuse to answer any of their questions. The boy did as he was told. He gave the two men the food and drink, then waited quietly

while they argued over how they should thank him. The men finally decided to reverse the order of the digits of the number of years Zao Yan was to live, thereby decreeing that he should live for a further 91 years. Zao Yan later discovered that one of the men had been Shou Lao.

SEMARA, according to the mythology of the Balinese, is the god of love who lives in the floating sky, one of a series of skies that lies above the layer of water hanging over the earth.

THE SAN XING Luxing and Fuxing are dressed as mandarins, while Shouxing, the god of longevity, holds a sprig of Ling Zhi, the plant of immortality. (JADEITE FIGURES, LATE QING DYNASTY.)

THE SAN XING (above) are usually portrayed as three good-humoured old men, surrounded by symbols of good fortune, longevity and immortality. (PAINTED SILK SCROLL BY WANG CHAO, C. 1500.)

SENGALONG BURONG see *SURONG GUNTING.*

SETESUYARA, according to Balinese mythology, is the goddess who rules over the underworld together with the god *BATARA KALA.*

SHAKA-NYORAI is the Japanese name for the Buddha Shakyamuni Gautama. Although Shaka is worshipped in Japan, the dominant form of Buddhism is the "Pure Land" school, whose followers chiefly venerate the buddha *AMIDA* or Amitabha.

SHANG DI, or Shang Ti, was worshipped as the ancestor of China's Shang dynasty, established around 1500 BC. The supreme god, he ruled over heaven and controlled natural phenomena such as

SHAKA-NYORAI, the Japanese buddha, preaching at Ryoj-Usen Mountain. (WALL PAINTING, 8TH CENTURY.)

the thunder, lightning, wind and rain. He was also regarded as the god of agriculture and was believed to determine people's fates. He was sometimes known simply as Di, which means "Lord" or "God".

SHANG TI see *SHANG DI.*

SHEN NONG, or Shen Nung, is an ancient Chinese god of medicine, health, agriculture and forestry. Together with *FU XI* and *HUANG DI*, he was one of the San Huang, or "Three Nobles", legendary emperors of China. He was sometimes referred to as the

"Divine Husbandman", although, as god of the hot winds, he could also bring harm. Shen Nong is said to have invented the plough to improve the lives of the ancient Chinese. He taught them how to grow food and revealed the medicinal properties of plants.

Because he had a transparent stomach, he was able to observe the effect of food and drink on his body. However, while investigating the effect of an unusual piece of grass, he turned black and died.

SHENG MU see *DONGYUE DADI.*

THE SHICHI FUKUJIN are the seven Japanese gods of good fortune or happiness. Their names are *DAIKOKU, EBISU, BENTEN,*

BISHAMON, FUKUROKUJU, JUROJIN and *HOTEI.* Among the group are deities from Buddhism, Japanese folklore and Chinese Daoism. The group was assembled in the 17th century by the monk Tenkai, who intended the gods to symbolize the virtues of fortune, magnanimity, candour, dignity, popularity, longevity and amiability. The deities are said to travel together on a treasure ship and are sometimes portrayed thus. (See also *THE SHICHI FUKUJIN*)

SHEN NONG (below left), with Huang Di, another legendary emperor of China.

SHEN NONG (below) is portrayed dressed in green leaves because he is a "primitive" deity and lived before clothes were ever invented.

SHOTEN, or Daisho-Kangiten, is a Japanese form of the Indian elephant-headed god Ganesha, who was adopted by certain Buddhist sects. His cult was introduced to Japan in the ninth century. Shoten both creates obstacles and overcomes them. He is worshipped by esoteric sects, and the god's tremendous power is believed to help people to gain enlightenment.

SHOU LAO is the Daoist god of long life. Originally known as Shouxing, he was one of the SAN XING or Chinese gods of good fortune. In due course, he came to rule over the department of the heavens that decrees the life-span of human beings. The god is usually shown with a large head and carrying a staff as well as a gourd, which holds the water of life. In his other hand, he holds the peach of eternal life. His creature is the white crane, a symbol of immortality. (See also THE EIGHT IMMORTALS)

SHOUXING see SHOU LAO.

SHUN is one of the five legendary emperors, or Wu Di, of Chinese mythology. The emperor YAO chose Shun, rather than his own son, as his successor. Shun was said to be a potter who travelled throughout the four directions and banished all the threatening creatures guarding their entrances. He is said to have lived in the third century BC and to have been succeeded by YU.

SUKU-NA-BIKONA, a dwarf deity, assisted OKUNINUSHI, one of Japan's great mythological heroes. He is regarded as a benevolent deity who is learned in both healing and cultivation.

After Okuninushi had settled in his palace with his wife, Suku-Na-Bikona arrived in a tiny boat on the crest of a wave. Okuninushi put the dwarf in the palm of his hand in order to examine him, whereupon the creature leapt up and bit the hero on his cheek. Okuninushi was

annoyed and told the gods what had happened. One of the gods realized that the dwarf must be his son, a mischievous child who had fallen to earth. The god asked Okuninushi to look after his child, who proceeded to help the hero to establish his rule. Eventually, however, Suku-Na-Bikona disappeared.

SURONG GUNTING is a culture hero of the Iban people of Borneo. He went to visit his grandfather, a spirit called Sengalong Burong and, during his journey, the stars taught him about the agricultural cycle. When he reached his destination, his grandfather taught him about rituals and omens.

SHOU LAO (left) wears the robes and hat of a mandarin in his capacity as the heavenly official who determines human life-spans. (CHINESE PORCELAIN, 18TH CENTURY.)

SHOU LAO (right), the Daoist god of long life, has a large head and carries a staff. (JADE CARVING, 17TH CENTURY.)

In due course Sengalong Burong threw the young man out of his house in punishment for having slept with his aunt, Dara Chempaka Tempurong. According to Sengalong Burong, if people of adjacent generations slept with one another there would be a terrible harvest. Surong Gunting returned to his home and taught his people all that he had learned.

SUSANO-WO is the storm god of Japanese Shinto mythology. He came into being when IZANAGI, the male half of the primal pair, washed his face after returning from the land of the dead. Susano-Wo emerged from Izanagi's nose.

Izanagi divided his kingdom between his three children, the others being the sun goddess AMATERASU and the moon god TSUKIYOMI. To Susano-Wo he allocated rulership of the ocean. Susano-Wo was dismayed with his lot and protested, saying that he wanted to join his mother IZANAMI in the underworld. Izanagi immediately banished Susano-Wo.

Before leaving, Susano-Wo visited his sister Amaterasu. He challenged her to a contest in order to determine which of them was the most powerful. The task was to see who of them could give rise to male deities. Susano-Wo took Amaterasu's fertility beads from her hair and arms and, breaking them with his teeth, blew them out as five male deities. He then pronounced himself victorious. Amaterasu disagreed, saying that the beads belonged to her, and therefore she had won the contest. Susano-Wo ignored his sister's protests and proceeded to celebrate

his victory by causing devastation on earth. He finished his riotous activities by throwing a flayed pony through the roof of the sacred weaving hall where Amaterasu sat with her attendants. Amaterasu was so angry that she hid in a cave, thereby bringing darkness to the world. Although Amaterasu was eventually lured out of the cave, the gods decided that Susano-Wo ought to be punished. They ordered him to give them numerous gifts and cut off his beard and the nails of his hands and feet. Finally, the gods threw Susano-Wo out of heaven.

According to another tale, Susano-Wo ordered the food goddess UKE-MOCHI to give him something to eat. The goddess responded by pulling food from her nose, mouth and rectum whereupon the disgusted Susano-Wo killed her. From her corpse sprouted all the basic food crops: rice seeds grew from her eyes, millet from her ears, wheat from her genitals, red beans from her nose

and soy beans from her rectum. In some versions of the legend, it is the moon god Tsukiyomi, rather than Susano-Wo, who kills the food goddess.

When Susano-Wo arrived on earth he set out to find some human beings. He soon came across an elderly couple and a beautiful young woman. The couple, weeping, told Susano-Wo that an eight-tailed, eight-headed monster called Yamato-no-Orochi had eaten seven of their eight daughters and was about to take their youngest daughter too. Susano-Wo promised to kill the monster and in return asked to be allowed to marry the daughter.

The couple agreed, whereupon Susano-Wo turned the daughter into a comb, which he fastened in his hair. The god then told the man and woman to place eight large

TAI SUI is surrounded by some of the 60 images which portray the annual Tai Sui. These are all subsidiary deities of the "Lord of Time".

tubs of rice wine on eight platforms and to surround the platforms with a fence containing eight openings. When the monster approached, it began to drink up the wine with its eight heads and soon fell down drunk. The god then chopped up the monster's body with his sword, discovering in the process the famous sword called Kusanagi or "Grass Mower" in its tail. (See also *CREATION MYTHS*)

SUSERI-HIME see *OKUNINUSHI*.

T'AI-I see *TAIYI*.

TAI SUI, the "President of the Celestial Ministry of Time" and "Ruler of the Year", is an arbiter of human destiny worshipped to avert calamities. He rules the cycle of 60 years, each of which is controlled by one of the subsidiary Tai Sui.

Astrology concerns human fortune, and the stellar deity Tai Sui presides over dates and times, auspicious or otherwise. Astrologers match a person's birth date and time with the cycle to provide a guide to auspicious and inauspicious years. Tai Sui was an early

deity honoured at the beginning of spring by the official religion and the official class in imperial China, as well as by Daoists. He is one of the fiercest gods in the pantheon and must be placated whenever ground is disturbed for any reason.

TAIYANG DIJUNG see *YI*.

TAIYI, or T'ai-i, has various meanings within Daoism. Sometimes it is said to be identical with the Dao, but over time it came to be personified as the highest deity within the Daoist pantheon. Taiyi is sometimes said to live in the polar star and to be served by the five mythical emperors.

TAIYI TIANZUN, or T'ai-i T'ientsun, is an early Daoist deity who is the saviour of sufferers and unfortunates. He is one of the more senior and significant of the Daoist gods, and is said to be equal to the "Jade Emperor" in rank.

Before the time of *HUANG DI*, the "Yellow Emperor", Taiyi Tianzun had been regarded as the supreme deity. He became the medical adviser to the "Yellow Emperor".

THE SHICHI FUKUJIN

SEVEN POPULAR JAPANESE DEITIES, the Shichi Fukujin, were considered to bring good luck and happiness. Each one personified a different aspect of good fortune. Although they were included in the Shinto pantheon, only two of them, Daikoku and Ebisu, were indigenous Japanese gods. Others were versions of popular Buddhist gods imported from China, while Benten and Bishamon originated as Hindu deities, and Hotei as a Daoist god. Buddhism was declared the official religion of the Japanese imperial court in AD 593, but instead of trying to stamp out the existing faith, Buddhist missionaries in Japan drew parallels between the two faiths and proclaimed the identities of the deities to be the same. Because of this peaceable marriage of the two faiths, it was easy for attractive and popular Buddhist gods, such as those of good fortune, to be assimilated with the innumerable kami of the old religion.

BISHAMON (above) the god of war, came from the Hindu pantheon. He stood for benevolent authority. He was a warrior and always wore full armour, so that he was forever ready for battle. He is always shown carrying a lance and a miniature pagoda to symbolize his dual virtues as a soldier and a missionary. (HERIAN PERIOD FIGURE, 11TH CENTURY.)

THE SEVEN GODS (above left) were often depicted travelling together on their treasure ship Takara-Bune, representing a cargo of all the good luck anyone could ask for in life. The ship carried various magical articles on board, such as a hat which rendered the wearer invisible, and a purse that was always full of money. (HIROSHIGE, TREASURE SHIP WITH SEVEN GODS OF GOOD FORTUNE, WOODBLOCK PRINT, 19TH CENTURY.)

BENTEN (left), the only goddess in the group of seven, was a goddess of love, and was believed to bring good luck in marriage. She rode on a dragon or a sea serpent and was associated with the sea, so her shrines were often located by the sea or on islands. She was a patron of music and played a stringed instrument called a biwa. (GILDED KOMAI BOX, LATE 19TH CENTURY.)

FUKUROKUJU (left), perhaps originally a Daoist sage, was the god of long life, wisdom and popularity. He was a little old man with a short body and legs and a very long, narrow bald head, which indicated his intelligence. His traditional companions were animals associated with longevity: a crane, a stag or a tortoise. (JAPANESE IVORY NETSUKE, 18TH CENTURY.)

HOTEI (left) was a fat, bald monk who carried a large sack and a small screen. His enormous belly was meant to indicate his contentment and serene good nature, rather than greed. He is often depicted seated comfortably on his sack, laughing merrily. (ARITA MODEL, LATE 17TH CENTURY.)

JUROJIN was the godson of Fukurokuju, and also promised long life and a happy old age. He had a long white beard to indicate his great age and was portrayed carrying a staff to which was attached a scroll containing all the wisdom of the world, including the life-span of each individual. (JAPANESE INRO, 19TH CENTURY.)

DAIKOKU was the god of wealth and agriculture. He was portrayed wearing a cap and hunter's clothes, surrounded by the symbols of prosperity. Standing or sitting on a bag of rice, he carried another large sack of rice over his shoulder and a rice mallet in his hand, with which he granted wishes. He was sometimes said to be the father of Ebisu. (SATSUMA MODEL, LATE 19TH CENTURY.)

EBISU was the Shinto god of work. The most popular of the seven gods, he was a fisherman, and was fat and cheerful. He was usually shown holding a large fish. Later, he became associated with profit and could bring good luck to commercial ventures. Ebisu was deaf, so he did not join the other gods for the Shinto festival at Izumo which takes place in October. Instead, his festival was held in his own temple. (SATSUMA MODEL, LATE 19TH CENTURY.)

TARVAA was one of the first shamans of Mongolia. As a young man, he fell ill, and his relatives assumed he was dead. Tarvaa was so displeased at this presumption that his soul left his body and flew up to the spirit world. There, he met the judge of the dead who demanded to know why he had arrived so early. The judge, impressed that the youth possessed the courage to visit his kingdom, offered to give him a present before he returned to the land of the living. Tarvaa, rather than choosing wealth or glory, asked to be given knowledge of all the marvels that he had encountered in the spirit world, together with the gift of eloquence. He then returned to his body. However, he found that in his absence, birds had pecked out his eyes, and so he spent the rest of his days unable to see. He became famous for his wisdom and his tales of the spirit world.

TAWARA-TODA is a hero, possibly of historic origins, who features in the mythology of Japan. He defeated an enormous centipede which had been ravaging the territory of the king of the dragons. In gratitude, the king gave Tawara-Toda several supernatural gifts, including a bag of rice which constantly refilled itself.

THE TENGRI, according to the mythology of the Buriats of Siberia, are a type of spirit being. It is said that 54 good-natured Tengri live in the west, whereas 45 bad-natured Tengri live in the east. The Tengri are also regarded as realms, all of which are interconnected, and which together form a cosmic tree.

THE TENGU are creatures of Japanese mythology who are said to live in trees and mountainous areas. Part human, part bird, they have long noses and are sometimes depicted wearing cloaks of feathers or leaves. Although they play tricks, they are not outrightly evil.

TEVNE, according to traditional Mongolian belief, is a hero who managed to appropriate the yellow book of divination from the king. The king had a beautiful daughter whom he desperately tried to protect by keeping her hidden from the outside world. All the king's servants knew that if they revealed the princess's whereabouts, the yellow book of divination would reveal their guilt. As a result, for many years the princess remained in hiding.

One day, Tevne decided that he would attempt to confuse the book. He dug a deep hole in the ground and trapped one of the princess's servants in it. He then built a fire on top of the hole, placed a kettle over the fire and, taking a piece of iron piping, passed it through the kettle. Then, speaking through the pipe, he asked the woman how he could find the princess. The woman told Tevne how the beautiful girl could be identified, so he released her.

Later, Tevne succeeded in picking out the princess from girls of similar appearance. Although the king was furious, he was forced to allow Tevne to marry her. In order

TIAN (above), the sky or heaven, is symbolized by a ceremonial Bi disc. (CHINESE JADE, 3RD–2ND CENTURY BC.)

THE TENGU (left), though wicked, could also be helpful, and rescued the hero Tameto from a giant fish. (WOODBLOCK PRINT BY KUNIYOSHI, 19TH CENTURY.)

to discover who had revealed the secret of his daughter's identity, the king sought advice from his yellow book. The book told him that he had been tricked by a man with earthen buttocks, a body of fire, lungs of water and an iron pipe for vocal cords. The king decided that the book's abilities had deserted it, and so he burned it. Sheep licked up the ashes and thereby acquired divinatory powers.

THE THENS, according to the people of Laos and northern Thailand, are the three divine ancestors who, together with three great men, Pu Lang Seung, Khun K'an and Khun K'et, established human society.

The Thens lived in the upper world, whereas the three great men ruled over the lower world, living by means of fishing and growing rice. A vast bridge joined together the two worlds.

One day, the Thens suddenly announced that all human beings should give them a portion of their food before they sat down to eat a meal. When the people refused, the Thens caused a huge flood to cover the earth. The three great men built a raft on top of which they constructed a house. Taking women and children with them, they travelled over the flood to the upper world in order to seek a reprieve from the chief Then.

The king of the Thens told the travellers to seek shelter in heaven with one of his relatives, Grandfather Then Lo. However, the three great men noticed that the flood was beginning to recede, and they told the king that they would rather return to the lower kingdom, since in heaven they were unable to walk or run because there was no solid ground. The king gave the divine ancestors a buffalo and sent them back down to earth.

Three years passed, after which time the buffalo died. A plant began to grow from its nostrils, and before long gave rise to three gourds. A strange noise issued from the gourds, whereupon one of the great men bored a hole in each of the fruit. Immediately, human beings began to emerge from the plants. The first people to emerge were the aboriginal slaves, followed in due course by the Thai people.

The three great men taught the people how to cultivate fields and how to weave. Later, Then Teng and Then Pitsanukukan descended from the upper world in order to teach the Thais about time as well as how to make tools, weave cotton and silk and prepare food.

Finally, the king of heaven sent the lord of the divine musicians to teach the people how to make and play instruments, and how to sing and dance. When the divine musician had finished his work he returned to heaven, and the bridge that connected the two worlds was destroyed.

TI see *SHANG DI.*

TI TS'ANG WANG see *DIZANG WANG.*

TIAN, or T'ien, is the Chinese word that refers both to the sky, or heaven, and to its personification as a deity. According to Daoism, there are 36 heavens, which are arranged on six levels. Each level is inhabited by different deities. The highest heaven is that of the "Great Web", which is sometimes said to be the home of the "Celestial Venerable of the Primordial Beginning", Yuanshi Tianzun.

From ancient times, Tian, or Tian Di, was regarded as a supreme being who had the power to influence the destiny of human beings, bringing order and calm, or catastrophe and punishment. The Chinese emperor is regarded as the "Son of Heaven", or Tianzi, and is believed to mediate between Tian and humankind.

TIAN DI see *TIAN.*

U

TIAN LONG see *DIYA*.

T'IEN see *TIAN*.

TING-JIAN see *GAO YAO*.

TOKOYO, according to Japanese mythology, was the daughter of a samurai called Oribe Shima who had displeased the emperor and been banished from the kingdom. Oribe Shima set up home on a desolate group of islands known as the Oki Islands.

He was extremely unhappy as he missed his daughter. Tokoyo was also miserable at being separated from her father and determined to find him. She sold all her property and set out for a place called Akasaki on the coast, from where the Oki Islands could just be seen. Although Tokoyo tried to persuade the fishermen to row her out to the islands, they all refused, since it was forbidden to visit anyone who had been sent there.

One night, Tokoyo took a boat and sailed out to the islands alone. She fell asleep on the beach, and the next morning she began to search for her father. The young woman soon encountered a fisherman and asked him if he had seen her father. He replied that he had not, and warned her not to ask anyone where he was as it might cause immense trouble. As a result, Tokoyo wandered all over the islands, listening to what people were saying, but never asking the whereabouts of her father.

One evening, she came to a shrine of the Buddha and after praying to him, fell asleep. She was soon woken by the sound of a girl crying and looking up she saw a young girl and a priest. The priest led the girl to the edge of the cliffs and was about to push her into the sea when Tokoyo ran up and stopped him. The priest confessed that he was forced to carry out the ritual in order to appease the evil god *OKUNINUSHI*. If he were not sent a young girl each year, the god

TOKOYO succeeded in killing a monstrous sea serpent and thus freed the emperor from an evil curse. (ILLUSTRATION FROM MYTHS AND LEGENDS OF JAPAN.)

would become very angry and cause great storms and many fishermen would drown.

Tokoyo offered to take the girl's place, saying that she was so unhappy without her father that the loss of her life meant nothing to her. Then, Tokoyo prayed to the Buddha again and, with a dagger between her teeth, dived into the ocean intending to hunt down the evil god and kill him.

At the bottom of the ocean, Tokoyo spied a marvellous cave. Inside, instead of the evil god, she found a statue of the emperor who had banished her father. She began to destroy the statue, but then thought better of it and, tying it to herself, she began to swim back. Just as she was leaving the cave, Tokoyo found herself confronted by

a serpentine creature. Unafraid, she swam up to it and stabbed it in the eye. Blinded, the creature was unable to gain entrance to the cave, and Tokoyo succeeded in attacking it until finally she killed it.

When Tokoyo arrived at the shore, the priest and the girl carried her to town, and word of her heroic deeds soon spread. The emperor himself, who had suddenly found himself cured of an unknown disease, heard what had happened and realized that Tokoyo must have released him from an evil spell. He ordered the release of Oribe Shima, and the father and daughter returned to their home town.

TOMAM, according to the Ket people of Siberia, is a goddess who looks after migratory birds.

TSAO-CHÜN see *ZAO JUN*.

TS'AO KUO-CHIU see *BA XIAN*.

TSUKIYOMI, in Shinto mythology, is the god of the moon. His name means "Counter of the Months". Tsukiyomi is said to have come into being when *IZANAGI*, the male half of the primal couple, purified himself after visiting the underworld. When he washed his face, Tsukiyomi appeared from Izanagi's right eye, the sun goddess *AMATERASU* from his left eye and the storm god *SUSANO-WO* from his nose. Izanagi divided his kingdom between his three offspring, allocating to Tsukiyomi the realms of the night.

According to one version of the myth relating how the staple crops of Japan were created, Tsukiyomi asked the food goddess *UKE-MOCHI* for a meal, but when she produced the food from her orifices, he was so disgusted that he killed her. The basic foodstuffs then appeared from the corpse of the goddess. When Amaterasu learned what had happened, she was displeased and said that she would never set eyes on her brother again. It is for this reason that the sun and the moon inhabit the sky at different times.

TUNG-YÜEH TA-TI see *DONGYUE DADI*.

UKE-MOCHI, or Ogetsu-No-Hime, is the food goddess, according to the Shinto mythology of Japan. She is married to *INARI*, the god of rice. The storm god *SUSANO-WO* or, in some versions of the story, the moon god *TSUKIYOMI* ordered the food goddess to give him something to eat. The goddess responded by pulling food from her nose, mouth and rectum

歸國
浦島

whereupon the god, disgusted, killed her. From Uke-Mochi's corpse sprouted all the basic food crops: rice seeds grew from her eyes, millet from her ears, wheat from her genitals, red beans from her nose and soy beans from her rectum. She is also said to have produced a cow and a horse.

ULGAN is the great sky god of the Altaic people of Siberia. He sent the saviour MAIDERE to earth in order to teach men to respect the true god. Maidere was slain by the evil ERLIK, but flames arose from his blood and reached up to heaven, destroying Erlik and his followers. Ulgan is sometimes depicted surrounded by rays of light.

ULU TOYO'N is the malevolent creator spirit of the Yakut people of Siberia. He lives in the third sky and rules over the ABAASY, evil beings who live in the lower world. Ulu Toyo'n is also the lord of thunder and is said to have given fire to human beings, as well as one of their three souls.

UMAI is the mother goddess of the Turkic people of Siberia. She is said to have 60 golden tresses, which resemble the rays of the sun, and to look after newborn babies and help couples to conceive. Sometimes known as Ymai, or Mai, she is believed to have originally been identical with OT, the fire queen of the Mongols.

URASHIMA was a young fisherman who features in the mythology of Japan. One day, when out fishing, he caught an old turtle. Rather than killing the creature, he took pity on it and threw it back into the water, whereupon a beautiful girl emerged from the spray. The girl stepped into Urashima's boat, told him that she was the daughter of the sea god, a dragon king, and invited him to come and live with her in their palace under the ocean. The palace was made of seashells, pearls and coral, and Urashima found himself waited upon by seven golden-tailed dragons.

For four years, Urashima lived in perfect happiness with his wife, the dragon princess. However, one day he began to long to see his parents and the streets where he used to play. Before he left for his former home, Urashima's wife gave him a casket, telling him that, provided it remained closed, it would enable him to return to her. When Urashima reached his homeland, he found that everything looked strange to him. Eventually, he

URASHIMA returned from his stay under the ocean riding on the back of a turtle.
(WOODBLOCK PRINT BY TAISO YOSHITOSHI, 1882.)

asked an old man if he knew the whereabouts of Urashima's cottage. The old man replied that Urashima had drowned 400 years ago while out fishing. Urashima was so shocked that he failed to remember his wife's instructions and opened the casket. Immediately, a puff of white smoke escaped from the casket and drifted towards the sea. Urashima himself suddenly began to grow old. His hair grew white and his hands shook, until finally he became no more than a pile of dust and was blown away on the wind.

USHIWAKA see YOSHITSUNE.

UZUME see AME-NO-UZUME.

WEN CHANG, the god of literature, is dressed as a mandarin and holds a sceptre as a symbol of his official position in the heavenly hierarchy. (CHINESE BLANC-DE-CHINE FIGURE, 17TH CENTURY.)

VIZI-ANYA see *VIZI-EMBER*.

VIZI-EMBER, according to the mythology of the Magyars of Siberia, is a water spirit who lives in lakes and rivers. He devours human beings and, if none are forthcoming, he will call out, demanding to be satisfied. Those who hear his voice know that someone is about to drown.

There are also two female water spirits, the water mother Vizi-anya and the water maiden Vizi-leany. Whenever one of these spirits appears to humankind, the vision signifies that something unfortunate is about to happen.

VIZI-LEANY see *VIZI-EMBER*.

WAKAHIRU-ME, according to Japanese Shinto belief, is the younger sister of the sun goddess *AMATERASU*. She is said to have been sitting with Amaterasu in the divine weaving hall when the storm god *SUSANO-WO* threw a flayed horse into the chamber.

The divine weaving hall was the place where Amaterasu and her attendants were said to weave garments, for the gods themselves or for the priestesses of the sun goddess. Alternatively, the deities were said to be weaving the unfinished parts of the universe.

WEN CHANG, the god of literature, is dressed as a mandarin and holds a sceptre as a symbol of his official position in the heavenly hierarchy. (CHINESE BLANC-DE-CHINE FIGURE, 17TH CENTURY.)

WATA RIAN, according to the Kedang people of eastern Indonesia, was the hero who civilized the wild woman *BOTA ILI*. Bota Ili lived on top of a mountain; her body was covered with hair and the nails of her fingers and toes were long and pointed. She ate lizards and snakes, and would cook them over a fire, which she lit by striking her bottom against a stone. One day, Wata Rian noticed the smoke of Bota Ili's fire and set off to find its source.

When he reached the top of the mountain, Wata Rian climbed a tree and waited for Bota Ili to return with her catch of reptiles. In due course, the wild woman returned. She struck her bottom against a rock to start a fire, but to no effect. Looking up, she saw Wata Rian and shrieked at him to come down from the tree in order that she might bite him to death. Wata Rian, unafraid, told her to calm herself or he would set his dog on her. The two of them lit a fire and cooked their food together. Bota Ili drank so much wine that she fell asleep, whereupon Wata Rian shaved the hair from her body and discovered that she was a woman. The couple were eventually married.

WEN CHANG is the Daoist god of literature. Originally a stellar deity, he descended from his home in the stars and lived through 17 lives, each of which was filled with remarkable events and achievements. At the end of this time, Wen Chang was finally rewarded by the "Jade Emperor" with the title "Grand Emperor of Literature".

THE WIND GOD is a nature spirit, like the gods of rain, thunder and lightning. He is portrayed as an old man carrying a sack of wind.

According to one story, a student was disappointed with his performance in an examination and, fearing he had failed, begged Wen Chang to help him. That night, while he was asleep, the student saw the god throwing several essays into a fire. Among them, the student recognized his own. After the essays had disintegrated into tiny pieces of ash, the god transformed them. Wen Chang gave the student his corrected essay, and the young man memorized it.

The following morning, the student discovered that a fire had destroyed the building where all the essays had been kept and that he would have to repeat the examination. This time, he wrote the essay as the god had instructed him and passed.

The deity is usually represented sitting down, wearing the robes of a mandarin and holding a sceptre. Wen Chang is in fact a constellation of six stars. When the stars are bright, literature is said to flourish. He is accompanied by several officials who set and mark exam papers and bear tidings to those who pass. They include *DIYA* and Tian Long.

THE WIND GOD, an impersonal nature deity, assumed human form as Feng Po during the Tang or Song dynasties. Images in mainland China portrayed him as an

elderly man carrying a sack of cold wind which he pointed in the direction he wished wind to blow. In northern and central China he was sometimes portrayed astride a tiger, and was also often depicted holding a pair of open fans with which he produced gentle breezes. He was accompanied by a shrimp spirit carrying a vase filled with rainwater which he sprinkled as he went.

THE WU DI, or Wu Ti, are the "Five Perfect Emperors" of Chinese mythology who are said to have lived during the third century BC. They are the "Yellow Emperor" (*HUANG DI*), Zhuan Xu, Du Gu, *YAO* and *SHUN*. One of the five elements is associated with each emperor.

XI-HE, or Hsi Ho, according to Chinese mythology, is the mother of the ten suns and the wife of Taiyang Dijun, the god of the eastern sky. Each morning, Xi-He would carry one of her sons to the edge of the sky in her chariot in order that he might spend the day lighting up the world. Eventually, the suns rebelled against their ordered existence and appeared in the sky together, thus causing devastation on earth. Nine of them were shot down by the divine archer *YI*.

XI WANG MU, or Hsi Wang-mu, is described in ancient Chinese texts as a monster with a human face, the teeth of a tiger and a leopard's tail. She ruled over the demons of the plague and was known as the goddess of epidemics. However, by the first century AD she had become a noble lady. Known as the "Queen Mother of the West", she was said to rule over the western paradise of the immortals in the Kunlun Mountains where she was attended by the "Jade Girls" and three-legged birds.

Xi Wang Mu is portrayed as a beautiful woman wearing a royal gown and sometimes riding on a crane. She is said to live in a palace of jade, nine storeys high and surrounded by a golden wall more than a thousand miles long. The male immortals live in the right wing of her palace and the female immortals in the left.

In her garden, Xi Wang Mu grows the peaches of immortality, which release all those who eat them from death. However, the tree bears fruit only once every 3,000 years. When the peaches are ripe, Xi Wang Mu invites all the immortals to a feast during which they eat the marvellous fruit.

Xi Wang Mu is said to have given a peach of immortality to several ancient Chinese rulers. In the myth of the divine archer *YI* and his wife *ZHANG E*, Yi is given the elixir of immortality by the "Queen Mother of the West", but Zhang E drinks it all up, thereby condemning her husband to life as a mortal. According to some versions of the tale of the immortal Li Tieguai, it was the Queen Mother of the West who taught him the secret of immortality.

In popular mythology, she is regarded as Wang Mu Niangniang, the wife of the "Jade Emperor", *YU HUANG*. Once a year, she is said to meet her consort, Dong Wang Gong, who lives in the east. The occasion is believed to symbolize the union of *YIN* and *YANG*.

XI WANG MU, with other deities, rides through the heavens in a celestial chariot drawn by cranes. (CAVE PAINTING AT DUNHUANG, CHINA, C. AD 535–556.)

DEMONS

DEMONS APPEARED IN ALL KINDS OF mythologies as servants and ministers of deities, including the ruler of the underworld. They usually personified forces of evil, and appeared on earth to wreak havoc among mortals by bringing disease and famine, or inhabiting the living. In the afterlife, they existed to punish the wicked with cruelly appropriate tortures for the sins they had committed in life. For a Buddhist, this state of torment could not be everlasting because rebirth continued, but the time in Naraka (the underworld) represented the lowest point of the soul's journey. In Japan, demons were called oni. Most were invisible, though some appeared in the form of animals, and they were the source of sin and misfortune. Even so, they were not viewed as wholly evil. The fox oni, for instance, was considered especially dangerous, yet was the companion of Inari, the rice god, who was popular and benevolent.

HELL (above) for the Chinese was divided into ten levels, presided over by the "Kings of the Law Courts". Souls had first to appear before Yanluo Wang, the supreme master, who heard their case then sent them on to each court in turn for their punishments to be decided. The kings, dressed like emperors, presided over the ghastly tortures that were carried out by demons. Souls could avoid hell only by living blameless lives and by making regular offerings to Guanyin, goddess of mercy. (ILLUSTRATION FROM SUPERSTITIONS EN CHINE, 1914.)

JIGOKUDAYU (left), the "Lady from Hell", was a Japanese courtesan who experienced enlightenment when she looked in her mirror and, instead of her reflection, saw a vision of a skeleton gazing back at her. She became a disciple of the 15th-century Zen master Ikkyu Sojun, the "Holy Madman" who frequented inns and brothels and danced in the street with a skull on a pole. Here, two laughing demons hold up a mirror for her to see her vision. (JIGOKUDAYU SEES HERSELF IN A MIRROR, BY TAISO YOSHITISHI, WOODBLOCK PRINT, 1882.)

BARONG (above) the spirit king, is the opponent of Rangda, the demon queen, in the great battle between good and evil, which is presented as a dance in Bali and other parts of South-east Asia. He takes the form of a lion, representing day, light and the forces of goodness. During their battle, the humans who try to help Barong are put under a spell by Rangda, which makes them turn their weapons on themselves, but Barong keeps them from harm. (BALINESE STONE CARVING.)

RANGDA (left), the ferocious female demon of Bali, had a lolling, fiery tongue, pendulous breasts and rolling eyes. A creature of darkness, sickness and death, she was the leader of a band of witches. Her name means "widow", and she may derive from an 11th-century Balinese queen exiled for practising sorcery. In revenge she tried to destroy the kingdom, and half the population died of plague before a holy man put an end to her black magic. (BALINESE RITUAL MASK.)

NAGAS (right) are dragon-like demons, and were dangerous and destructive spirits. Of Indian origin, their mythology spread with Buddhism into China and beyond. Some are half-human, half-snake, while others are monstrous water creatures who guard the depths of lakes. Naga Padoha is the serpent ruler of the underworld who, according to the mythology of South-east Asia, was confined there by the creator god Batara Guru when he tried to destroy the earth. (NAGA SCULPTURE IN A BALINESE SHRINE FOUNTAIN.)

Y

THE XIAN were said to live in the Kunlun Mountains, the location of the sacred peach garden where Xi Wang Mu, the "Queen Mother of the West", grew the peaches of immortality which they ate to ensure eternal life. (PAINTING, C 14TH CENTURY.)

THE XIAN, or Hsien, according to Chinese mythology, are beings who have gained immortality. They are not deities, but have been granted the gift of eternal life.

The immortals are either celestial or terrestrial. Celestial immortals live in Tian, the Daoist heaven, or on the isles of the immortals situated in the Eastern Sea, or in the Kunlun Mountains. They can change their appearance at will and are often represented riding on the backs of cranes. The terrestrial immortals live in forests and mountains.

XUAN ZANG, or Hsüan Tsang, was a celebrated Buddhist monk of the seventh century AD. Said to have been commissioned by the emperor of China, he journeyed to the source of Buddhism in India in quest of instruction, and returned with Buddhist scriptures. Some of his bones are still revered in temples in China and Japan.

Xuan Zang's great pilgrimage was immortalized in the 16th-century novel *Xi You Ji* (*The Journey to the West*) by Wu Zheng-en. According to this story, the monk was accompanied by four aides on his hazardous journey. Of the four, the most important and active was the "Monkey King". The other three were part players, the illiterate and slow-witted monk Sha; Piggy; and the White Horse on which Xuan Zang rode.

YA-GAMI-HIME see *YAKAMI*.

YAKAMI, or Ya-Gami-Hime, was a beautiful princess of Japanese mythology who lived at Inaba, a province near Izumo. The 80 brothers of the great hero *OKUNINUSHI* all wished to marry the princess. On their way to woo her, they met a hare that had been flayed. The brothers cruelly advised the hare to cure itself by bathing in the sea and drying itself in the wind. Naturally, this caused the animal to suffer severe pain. Later, when Okuninushi came across the hare, he told it to bathe in fresh water and then roll in the pollen of kama grass. On doing so, the hare found itself cured. It revealed itself to be a deity and told Okuninushi that he would marry Yakami.

YAKUSHI-NYORAI was one of the first buddhas to be venerated in Japan and became one of the most important. While still a bodhisattva, he is said to have made 12 vows, including promising to find a cure for all illnesses.

His name means "Master with Remedies", and he is commonly known as the "King of Medicines", or the "Divine Healer". Yakushi also vowed to transform his body into beryl in order that he might light up the whole world with his radiance. His home, situated in the east, was known as the "Land of Pure Beryl".

Yakushi-Nyorai is usually shown carrying a medicine bowl, and miraculous powers are attributed to his effigies.

THE XIAN included figures such as Han Shan, one of "The Four Sleepers" who is usually depicted holding a scroll. He would explain its contents to his fellow sleeper, Shi De, in unintelligible gibberish. (PAINTED SILK SCROLL, 14TH CENTURY.)

YAMATO TAKERU is a hero who features in the mythology of Japan. Originally called O-Usu-No-Ikoto, he was the son of Emperor Keiko. The emperor told his other son to bring two beautiful young women to him, but the son made the maidens his own wives and sent two other women in their place. The emperor, who was planning to punish his son, ordered Yamato Takeru to bring his brother to dine.

After five days, there was still no sign of the brother. Puzzled, the emperor asked Yamato Takeru what had happened to him. Yamato replied that he had crushed his brother to death and pulled off his limbs. The emperor, impressed at his son's strength, sent Yamato Takeru to destroy some rebels who threatened his kingdom.

For his first quest, the hero was sent to the west to slaughter two brothers. The palace of the brothers was surrounded by countless

warriors, so Yamato Takeru disguised himself as a girl and entered the palace during a feast. While everyone was busy eating and drinking, Yamato Takeru caught hold of one of the brothers and stabbed him. The other brother tried to escape, but Yamato Takeru seized and killed him, too. As the second brother lay dying, he named his killer Yamato Takeru or "Brave One of the Yamato".

On his journey home, Yamato Takeru brought all the mountain, river and sea deities under control. However, he had not been at home long when the emperor sent him off on another mission. Yamato Takeru complained to his aunt Yamato Pime that he needed time to rest, as well as more protection, and so his aunt gave him a sword and a bag, which she told him to open only in an emergency. The hero then did as his father, the emperor, had asked and killed many more enemies.

Eventually, a man lured Yamato Takeru into a trap. He begged the hero to go to a pond in the middle of a vast plain and kill a deity who lived in its waters. Once Yamato Takeru was in the middle of the plain, the man set fire to the area, trapping the hero. Undeterred,

Yamato Takeru cut down the grass with his magic sword. Then, opening the bag his aunt had given him, the hero found it contained a flint. Immediately, he lit another fire, which overcame the first, killing the man and all his followers.

Yamato Takeru performed many other brave and glorious deeds. On his long homeward journey, while crossing the sea in a boat with his wife Oto Tatiban Pime or Miyazu-Hime, the sea deity began to stir up the waves. Oto Tatiban Pime offered to sacrifice herself in order to save her husband and, stepping out of the boat, disappeared beneath the waves. Once on shore again, Yamato Takeru broke his journey by a mountain pass in order to eat some food. Seeing a deer, the hero threw the remains of his meal at the animal, not realizing that it was the deity of the pass. The deer fell down dead. Soon afterwards, Yamato Takeru encountered another deity in the form of a white boar and broke a taboo by saying that he would kill it. A fearsome hailstorm then descended, dazing the hero. None the less, Yamato Takeru struggled onwards until eventually he fell down dead. His soul was transformed into a huge white bird.

XUAN ZANG (above), the fabled travelling monk, is accompanied by his aides, the Monkey King, Piggy, the slow-witted She and the White Horse.

YAKUSHI-NYORAI (below) is the "Divine Healer" of Japanese Buddhism. Effigies of the buddha are credited with miraculous curative powers. (GILT BRONZE, 8TH CENTURY.)

YAN DI see *SHEN NONG*.

YAN WANG see *YANLUO WANG*.

YANG, according to Daoist belief, originally stood for the mountain slope facing the sun, and was associated with light and warmth. This ancient concept came to be viewed as one of the two cosmic forces, the other being *YIN*, which interacted to produce the universe. Yang represents masculinity, activity, heat, dryness and hardness. It is believed that yang may have originally been a sky deity. (See also *YIN AND YANG*)

YANLUO WANG is the senior king of the ten courts of the Chinese underworld. He investigates the past lives of the dead and sends them on to the other kings for punishment in the hells which are attached to each court. Eight of the "Kings of the Law Courts" punish particular souls while the remaining king allocates souls to bodies in preparation for their reincarnation. However, according to some versions of the tale, every soul has to appear before each of the courts in turn.

Horrific tortures await serious offenders: corrupt officials are forced to swallow molten gold, and the worst offenders are plunged into boiling oil, crushed by stones or cut in half.

YAO is one of the five legendary emperors of Chinese mythology. He is said to have ruled over China during the third century BC. Within Confucianism, Yao is regarded as the examplar of a good ruler. He is credited with having established the calendar, and with introducing official posts whose holders were responsible for making correct use of the four seasons of the year.

It was during his reign that the divine archer *YI* shot nine of the ten suns out of the sky and that a huge flood threatened to destroy the world. Yao made *SHUN* his succes-

sor, subjecting him to a series of tests before allowing him to take over the reins of power.

YI is the divine archer of Chinese mythology. He performed many brave deeds, including shooting nine of the ten suns from the sky, obtaining the elixir of immortality from *XI WANG MU*, and bringing under control the winds which plagued the "Yellow Emperor".

The ten suns lived in a giant mulberry tree known as Fu Sang, which grew in a hot spring beyond the eastern ocean. They were the children of Taiyang Dijun, the god of the east and lord of heaven, and *XI-HE*, goddess of the sun. Xi-He ordained that only one sun should appear in the sky at a time so, each morning, she would drive a sun to the edge of the sky in her chariot,

and at the end of the day would return it to the Fu Sang tree. In this way, light and warmth were brought to the world.

After a thousand years, the ten suns grew tired of their ordered way of life and decided to rebel. One day, they all appeared in the sky together. They were delighted with themselves, but their continual presence in the sky caused devastation on earth: the soil dried up, the crops withered and died and even the rocks began to melt. Soon there was scarcely anything left to eat or drink. Monsters and wild animals came out of the forest in search of food and began to devour human beings.

Eventually, the people begged their ruler, *YAO*, to help them. Yao prayed to Taiyang Dijun to take pity on humankind. Taiyang Dijun and

YANLUO WANG is the terrifying king of hell who presides over the judgement and punishment of souls. (CHINESE CERAMIC, 1523.)

Xi-He heard Yao's prayers and ordered nine of the suns to return to the Fu Sang tree. However, their entreaties fell on deaf ears.

Taiyang Dijun then called on the divine archer Yi for help. The great god gave Yi a red bow and a quiver of white arrows, and told him to bring his sons under control and to kill the wild animals. Yi, together with his wife *ZHANG E*, proceeded to do as Taiyang Dijun had instructed him. However, whereas Dijun had intended Yi merely to frighten the suns into submission, Yi decided that the only solution was to kill them. Taking an arrow from his quiver, he fired it high into the sky. Immediately, a huge ball of

fire appeared, and the air was filled with flames. On the ground lay a three-legged raven. Yi then shot another arrow at the sky, and another; each time, one of the suns was extinguished and fell to earth as a three-legged raven.

Yao realized that if Yi carried on, no light or warmth whatsoever would be left, so he told one of his courtiers to steal one of Yi's arrows so that he could destroy only nine of the ten suns. When there was only one sun left in the sky, Yi began to kill the wild animals and monsters that were devouring human beings.

Peace returned to the earth, and everyone praised Yi. The divine archer returned to heaven with Zhang E. However, to Yi's surprise, and Zhang E's anger, the god Taiyang Dijun spurned Yi for having killed his sons and ordered him and his wife to leave heaven and live on earth as mortals.

Yi was happy enough, hunting in the forests, but Zhang E grew bored and worried that now, one day, she would die. As a result, Zhang E persuaded Yi to visit the "Queen Mother of the West" and ask her for the elixir of immortality. The Queen Mother agreed to help

Yi and Zhang E. She gave them a box containing enough elixir to enable them to live for ever, but said that there was only sufficient elixir for one of them to gain complete immortality.

Zhang E swallowed all of the elixir herself, and was punished by being stranded on the moon. When Yi discovered his wife's treachery, he was dismayed. However, he decided that, since he was to die, he should pass on his skills. He took a pupil, Peng Meng, who soon became an expert archer, although not so proficient as Yi. In time, Peng Meng grew jealous of Yi's superior ability and killed him. Another version tells how Yi was finally forgiven by the gods and returned to heaven.

YIN, according to Daoist belief, originally referred to the mountain slope facing away from the sun. Together with *YANG*, Yin was viewed as one of the two cosmic forces whose interaction produced the universe. Yin represents the female principle – the cold, the dark and softness – and may have originated as an earth deity. (See also *YIN AND YANG*).

YINGZHOU see *PENG LAI*.

YINLUGEN BUD, the ghost of the tree trunk, is an ancient spirit of the Chewong people of Malaysia. He taught the hero *BUJAEGN YED* how to deliver children and instructed him in many other rituals associated with childbirth. He also warned Bujaegn Yed that it was sinful not to share his food when he ate a meal.

YMAI see *UMAI*.

YNAKHSYT see *ITCHITA*.

YOMI is the land of the dead in Japanese Shinto mythology. It is a land of filth rather than of punishment, and it is known as the "Land of Darkness", or the "Land of Roots". *IZANAGI*, the male half of the primal couple, followed his wife *IZANAMI* to Yomi, but failed to secure her release.

YOSHITSUNE, also known as Ushiwaka, is a hero who features in Japanese mythology. He was trained in the art of warfare by the Tengu and then succeeded in

YAO, fourth of the legendary emperors of China, was the pattern of the good ruler. (PAINTING BY MA LIN.)

YOSHITSUNE was trained in swordplay by the Tengu, the bird-like imps of Japanese myth. (WOODBLOCK PRINT BY KUNISADA, C. 1815.)

avenging the defeat of his people, the Minamoto clan. He defeated the giant *BENKEI* in a duel whereupon the giant became his servant.

YU was the hero of the flood in Chinese mythology. He is revered for his dedication to hard work. Yu was sometimes shown as half-dragon, half-human, but eventually he came to be represented as entirely human.

Yu laboured for 13 years to put an end to the flood. He controlled and directed all the waters of the earth by cutting holes through the mountains, creating rivers, springs and estuaries. Eventually, his hands and feet grew callused, and he became so exhausted, he could scarcely walk. However, he struggled on, building an irrigation system in order to drain the flood waters into the sea.

In the course of his mammoth drainage work, he made the land fit for cultivation and connected the nine provinces of China to one another. The ruling emperor was so grateful that he abdicated and gave the throne to Yu, who became the first emperor of the Xia dynasty. Yu is said to have reigned from 2205 to 2197 BC. Each succeeding emperor was seen as an incarnation of the dragon Yu.

Another myth tells how, in order to carry out his work, Yu would transform himself into a bear. Each day, when the time came for him to eat, he would beat his drum, and his wife would carry out food for him. One day, when Yu was breaking up rocks, his wife

YU HUANG (above), the "Jade Emperor" or "August Personage of Jade" is the supreme ruler of heaven and earth.

mistook the sound for the beating of his drum. She rushed out with his food, but as soon as she saw the bear she fled. Yu ran after her but, being pregnant, she fell to the ground exhausted and turned to stone. The stone continued to grow and, when the time of the expected birth arrived, Yu split it open, whereupon his son, Qi, was born.

YU DI was another name given to *YU HUANG*, the so-called "Jade Emperor" of Chinese mythology.

YU HUANG, or the "Jade Emperor", came to be regarded as the supreme ruler of heaven in Chinese mythology. He was responsible for determining events both in the heavens and on earth, and he had a vast number of underlings to carry out his commands. Yu Huang's chief assistant was *DONGYUE DADI*, or "Great Emperor of the Eastern Peak". Dongyue Dadi alone had 75 gods to help him in his work.

At the beginning of each year, Yu Huang would summon all the deities to his palace, which was in

YU (left) the Lord of the Flood, was given the task of controlling and draining the waters that covered the plains of China.

is usually depicted sitting on his throne wearing the ceremonial robes of an emperor, embroidered with dragons.

The "Queen Mother of the West", *XI WANG MU*, who is known by many titles, including Wang Mu Niangniang, was said to be the wife of Yu Huang. He has a large family of sisters, daughters and nephews, and a celestial dog, who helps to protect the heavenly household from evil spirits.

YUANSHI TIAN-ZONG see *SAN QING DAOZU*.

YUQIANG, or Yü-ch'iang, in Chinese mythology, is the god of the sea and of ocean winds. As a

god of the sea, he is represented with the body of a fish and riding two dragons. As a god of the winds, he is represented with the body of a bird and a human face.

According to one tale, Yuqiang was ordered by the king of heaven to anchor the five floating islands of the immortals. Yuqiang succeeded in the task by enlisting the help of 15 giant tortoises. He allocated three of the tortoises to each island and ordered them to take it in turns to carry one of the islands on their backs. Each turn was to last 60,000 years. Unfortunately, a giant caught six of the tortoises, and so two islands were set adrift. They floated away and sank, leaving only three.

QING LONG PA JIANG JUN, (left) The Green Dragon General, who guards the entrance to the Jade Emperor Hall.

YUQIANG (below), the god of the ocean winds, listens to the Buddhist doctrine. (PAINTING BY ZHAO BOZHU, SONG DYNASTY.)

the highest of the heavens, and was guarded by the "Transcendental Official". The deities would then be allocated new positions, according to how they had performed their duties during the previous year. The various ministries oversaw everything, from water and time, to war and wealth.

The heavenly administration was a replica of the earthly one. If, for example, there was a flood, the earthly official would warn the heavenly official – the deity – that his work was substandard and, if necessary, he would be fired. New deities would be confirmed by the Daoist priests. The "Jade Emperor" was said to deal directly with the emperor of China, whereas his attendants dealt with less important human beings. In the 11th

century AD, when the emperor of China was losing his power, he attempted to regain support by claiming to be in direct communication with heaven and to have received a letter from Yu Huang.

One myth tells how before Yu Huang was born, his mother dreamt that *LAO JUN*, the deified form of Laozi, the putative founding father of Daoism, handed her a child. The young Yu Huang succeeded his father, the king, to the throne but abdicated after a few days in order to retire to the mountains and study the Dao. He attained perfection and, for the rest of his life, he instructed the sick and poor in the Dao. Eventually, he became an immortal and after millions more years was transformed into the "Jade Emperor". Yu Huang

CHINA'S SACRED PEAKS

THE GREAT CREATOR PANGU lived for 18,000 years, growing every day and filling the space between the earth and the sky. When he died, his body formed the world. In one version of the myth, his head became Tai Shan mountain in the east; his feet, Hua Shan in the west; his right arm, the northern Heng Shan; his left arm, the southern Heng Shan; and his stomach Song Shan, the mountain of the centre. These were the five sacred Daoist mountains of China. They were worshipped as deities in their own right: pilgrims climbed stairways to the summits and made sacrifices to them. In the heavenly bureaucracy of the Chinese pantheon, the "Ministry of the Five Sacred Mountains" was controlled by Tai Shan, the grandson of Yu Huang, the "Jade Emperor".

TAI SHAN's (above) summit is reached by climbing the "Stairway to Heaven", which consists of about 7,000 steps lined with shrines and temples. Sacrifices were offered at the top of the mountain by the emperor each spring, but he could not presume to do this unless his reign was a successful one. Successive emperors made ceremonial journeys to the holy mountains that marked the limits of the empire, to assert their claim to their territory.

TAI SHAN (left), the holiest peak, is the sacred mountain of the east. Its presiding deity ("Lord of the Yellow Springs") ruled the earth and regulated birth and death, while his daughter Bixia Shengmu ("Princess of Streaked\Clouds") protected women and children. Souls left the mountain at birth and returned there at death. The mountain was granted various noble titles by the Jade Emperor.

A PAGODA (right) stands at the summit of Mount Song Shan, the mountain of the centre, in the heart of the ancient Chinese empire.

HUANG DI (below left) the "Yellow Emperor", was the third and most splendid of the legendary emperors of China, preceded by Fu Xi and Shen Nong. Huang Di ordered roads to be built and mountain passes to be cut throughout his empire. When he journeyed to Tai Shan to make sacrifices, his chariot was drawn by six dragons. Tigers and wolves preceded it, serpents slithered beside it, phoenixes flew overhead and spirits followed behind. The road ahead was cleaned and swept by the gods of wind and rain.

HUA SHAN (above) was the sacred mountain of the west. The hero Yu, who controlled the great flood of China, visited the four corners of the world, marked by the sacred peaks. At Hua Shan he found people who drank dew and ate the air, who had three faces each but only one arm. Daoists believed that mountain-tops brought them closest to the Dao and built many of their temples on or near the summits of the sacred mountains.

HENG SHAN (left) in Shanxi Province, has a monastery clinging precariously to the sheer rock face. This is the northern Heng Shan, said to have been formed from the right arm of the giant Pangu.

ZAO JUN, or Tsao-chun, is a Daoist kitchen god, worshipped since at least the second century BC. He is still widely worshipped, and his picture is placed above the kitchen stove. At New Year, his spirit is offered a meal of meat, fruit and wine, and his lips are smeared with honey. The portrait is then burned in order to help the god on his way to heaven. The honey is supposed to keep Zao Jun sweet for when he reports on each family's conduct to *YU HUANG*.

According to one story, Zao Jun was once a poor man who, because he was unable to support his wife,

or because of a trick she played on him, had to allow her to marry someone else. He wandered far and wide begging. One day, he realized he had come to the home of his former wife and was so ashamed that he tried to hide in the hearth, where he was burned to death.

Another version of the tale tells how, before he became a deity, Zao Jun was a man called Zhang Lang. He was married to a good and faithful woman but left her for a young girl. Things went badly for him. In due course, the young girl became bored with Zhang Lang; he lost his sight and had to beg for food.

One day, Zhang Lang appeared at the door of his former wife. However, being blind, he did not know her. The woman invited Zhang Lang in and gave him his favourite meal. He was reminded of his wife and told the apparent stranger his story. His wife told Zhang Lang to open his eyes, and when he did so, he found he was able to see again. However, Zhang Lang was so ashamed at his former behaviour that he jumped into the hearth and was burned to death. His wife managed to seize one of his legs, which is why the fire poker is described as "Zhang Lang's leg".

ZAO JUN, the kitchen god, is honoured with fire crackers during the New Year celebrations. (CHINESE PAINTING, 19TH CENTURY.)

ZHANG E, or Chang O, according to Chinese mythology, is the wife of the divine archer *YI*. The lord of heaven, Taiyang Dijun, condemned Yi and Zhang E to live on earth as mortals in punishment for killing nine of his ten sons. Zhang E was furious and persuaded Yi to obtain the elixir of immortality from *XI WANG MU*, who lived on Mount Kunlun. The myth varies slightly, but, according to one version, the Queen Mother took pity

月宮 睹嫦奔月

down a tree. According to one version of the myth, Zhang E did finally regain her human appearance and lived the rest of her life in the palace of the moon. She is often shown wearing regal garments and carrying the disc of the moon in her right hand. She is regarded as a symbol of *YIN*, the female principle.

ZHANG GUOLAO see *BA XIAN*.

ZHONG-LI QUAN see *BA XIAN*.

ZHU RONG, or Chu Jong, according to Chinese mythology, is regent of the southern quarter of heaven and the divine lord of fire. He helped to divide heaven and earth from each other. One myth tells how Zhu Rong and the ferocious monster *GONG-GONG* decided to fight each other in order to determine which of them was the most powerful. Zhu Rong managed to defeat Gong-gong, who was so ashamed that he tried to kill himself and in the process caused a massive flood.

ZHU RONG (below), *the God of Fire, on a temple altar in Taipei, Taiwan.*

on Yi and gave him enough elixir to enable two people to live for ever, but only sufficient for one person to gain complete immortality. Yi returned home with the elixir, and Zhang E immediately began to toy with the idea of swallowing all the elixir herself. However, she was worried that the gods might be angry with her if she abandoned her husband, so she consulted an astrologer. The astrologer suggested that Zhang E should travel to the moon where she would be free both from the accusations of the gods and the hardships of life as a mortal. He also promised that Zhang E would be miraculously transformed.

Zhang E was immediately persuaded by the astrologer's suggestion. She stole the elixir of immortality from where it was hidden in the rafters of her house and swallowed it. Immediately, she began to float up to the moon. However, when she tried to call out, she discovered that she could only croak: she had been transformed into a toad.

Zhang E's companions on the moon were a hare and an old man who constantly attempted to chop

FAMILY TREE

SHINTO CREATION MYTH

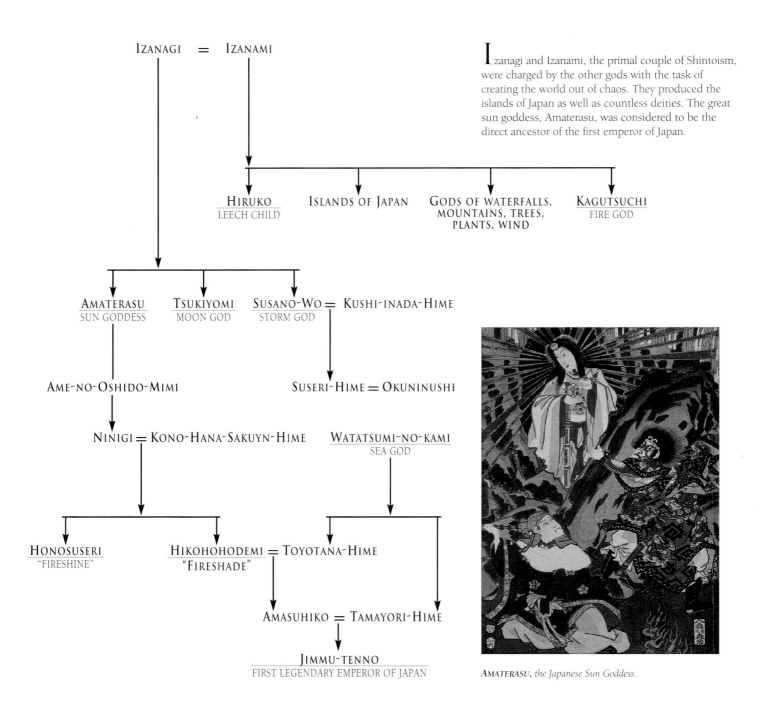

Izanagi = Izanami

HIRUKO
LEECH CHILD

ISLANDS OF JAPAN

**GODS OF WATERFALLS,
MOUNTAINS, TREES,
PLANTS, WIND**

KAGUTSUCHI
FIRE GOD

AMATERASU
SUN GODDESS

TSUKIYOMI
MOON GOD

SUSANO-WO = KUSHI-INADA-HIME
STORM GOD

AME-NO-OSHIDO-MIMI

SUSERI-HIME = OKUNINUSHI

NINIGI = KONO-HANA-SAKUYN-HIME

WATATSUMI-NO-KAMI
SEA GOD

HONOSUSERI
"FIRESHINE"

HIKOHOHODEMI = TOYOTANA-HIME
"FIRESHADE"

AMASUHIKO = TAMAYORI-HIME

JIMMU-TENNO
FIRST LEGENDARY EMPEROR OF JAPAN

Izanagi and Izanami, the primal couple of Shintoism, were charged by the other gods with the task of creating the world out of chaos. They produced the islands of Japan as well as countless deities. The great sun goddess, Amaterasu, was considered to be the direct ancestor of the first emperor of Japan.

AMATERASU, *the Japanese Sun Goddess.*

CHRONOLOGY

10,000-300 BC	Japanese Jomon culture. Hunter-gatherers living in settled villages: evidence of pottery and polished stone tools.
5000-2700 BC	Chinese Yangshao culture: evidence of rice cultivation and basketry.
3500-2000 BC	Chinese Longsham culture: domestication of cattle and sheep.
3rd millennium BC	Reigns of Fu Xi, Shen Nong and Huang Di.
2205-1766 BC	Xia dynasty
2205-2197 BC	Reign of Yu, first emperor of the Xia dynasty, though no archaeological evidence confirms this.
1766-1027 BC	Shang dynasty
1766 BC	Chinese state established by the Shang kings along the Yellow River. Shang culture includes the casting of bronze and the practice of ritualized human sacrifice.
By 14th century BC	Writing and art have developed in China.
1384 BC	City of Anyang is founded and becomes burial site of Shang kings.
1027-771 BC	Western Zhou dynasty
1027 BC	Zhou invaders led by Wu-wang overthrow the last Shang ruler, Di Xin.
771-249 BC	Eastern Zhou dynasty
771 BC	The Chinese king Yu is killed by his alienated nobles, who install a new leader, Ping, and move the capital east to Luoyang.
790-481 BC	Chinese Spring and Autumn period
7th century BC	Chinese feudal system breaks down and central authority collapses.
551-479 BC	Life of Kong Fuzi, founder of Confucianism, which emphasizes the importance of filial piety and respect for authority.
6th century BC	Life of Laozi, author of the Dao-de Jing, which forms the basis of Daoism.
481-221 BC	Chinese Warring States period

479-438 BC	Life of the philosopher Mozi, founder of Mohism, which advocates centralized government on strictly rational principles, uniformly applied standards and advancement through merit.
4th century BC	Development of the cross-bow in China means that battles are no longer fought between nobles in chariots, but with large armies of foot-soldiers.
373-288 BC	Life of the Confucian philosopher and sage, Mengzi (Mencius), who believes in innate human goodness but considers that rebellion against an immoral ruler may be justified.
320-235 BC	Life of the philosopher Xunzi, founder of Legalism, which argues that human beings are innately evil and must be ruthlessly controlled.
316 BC	Qin forces conquer Szechuan.
300 BC-AD 300	Japanese Yayoi culture: agricultural society using bronze and iron.
3rd century BC	A new legal code stratifies Chinese society in four tiers: lesser nobility (including scholars), farmers, artisans and merchants, and organizes households into groups to control one another's behaviour.
221-206 BC	Qin dynasty

2nd century BC	Deification of Laozi, founder of Daoism.
154 BC	Emperor Han Jing Di changes Chinese inheritance law, making all sons co-heirs of their father's estate, so that large holdings are broken down and the power of the aristocracy is reduced.
138 BC	A Chinese envoy visits the Indo-Greek kingdom of Bactria (in modern Afghanistan) and discovers that China is not the only civilization in the world.
124 BC	Foundation of the Chinese Imperial University.
119 BC	Chinese merchants are forbidden to own land, and the iron and salt industries become monopolies owned by the state.
9-25 AD	Xin dynasty
25-220	Eastern Han dynasty
50-70	Buddhism spreads to China.
105	Paper-making begins in China.
184	Rebellion of the Yellow Turbans, against the Chinese Han dynasty, weakens its power. The soldier-poet, Cao Cao, assumes authority in all but name, and his son becomes the first Wei emperor.
220-280	Chinese period of the Three Kingdoms
220	China is divided into three separate states, Wei, Wu and Shu.
280-316	Western Jin dynasty
300-710	Japanese Kofun period
317-589	Tartar partition of China
5th century	Bodhidharma establishes the Chan, or Zen, school of Buddhism in China.
5th century	Writing is introduced to Japan from Korea.
c 511	Emperor Liang Wudi, a Buddhist, invites 3000 Indian monks to China and establishes a translation school for Buddhist texts at Nanjing.
c 552	Buddhism is introduced to Japan from Korea.

221 BC	The Warring States period ends with Qin victorious. China is unified under the first Qin emperor, Qin Shihuang Di. All noble families are compelled to live in Xianyang, the Chinese capital. A single bureaucracy is instituted and laws, currency, writing, weights and measures are all standardized.
214 BC	Building of the Great Wall of China begins, to keep the nomadic Xiongnu out, and the Chinese population in.
213 BC	Emperor Qin Shihuang Di orders all Chinese books except those on medicine, agriculture and divination to be burnt, to quell criticism of his rule from Confucian scholars.
206 BC	The Chinese imperial library is burnt down: sole surviving copies of classic texts destroyed.
206 BC-AD 8	Western Han dynasty

589-619	Sui dynasty
593	Buddhism is declared the official religion of the Japanese court.
604-701	Taika reform of Japanese law and government, modelled on the Chinese Tang dynasty.
619-907	Tang dynasty
620-649	Tibet is unified under King Songsten Gampo and poses a threat on China's western frontier.
7th-9th centuries	Golden age of Chinese artistic achievement, especially of poetry and fine art. The earliest known printed book dates from 868.
c 640	Emperor Tai Zong commissions a Sanskrit translation of the Dao-de Jing to spread Daoist teachings westward.
690-705	Reign of Wu Ze Tian (Sheng Shen), China's only female ruler.
710-94	Japanese Nara period
710	First permanent Japanese capital is established at Heijo-kyo (Nara).
724-749	Reign of Japanese Emperor Shomu, who orders the construction of a Buddhist temple, monastery and nunnery in every province.
749	Shomu declares the laws of Buddha and Japanese imperial edicts to be identical.
c 750	Java is invaded by the Sailendra dynasty of Srivijaya, Sumatra.
768	A Buddhist temple is built at the shrine of Amaterasu, Shinto's holiest site.
794-1184	Japanese Heian period
794	The Japanese capital is moved to Heian-kyo (Kyoto) by Emperor Kanmu, to limit the powers of the Buddhist clergy.
9th century	Construction of Borobudur, Java.
802-1440	Khmer period in Cambodia

805	Saicho founds the Tendai school of Buddhism in Japan.
845-846	Suppression of Buddhism in China: 44,000 shrines and monasteries are closed.
889-910	Reign of Yasovarman I in Cambodia, who builds his capital at Angkor.
907-960	Collapse of central Chinese government.
960-1127	Northern Song dynasty
11th century	Beginning of mechanized industry in China.
c 1010	The Tale of Genji is written by Murasaki Shikibu.
1016-1087	King Munjong of Korea commissions the printing of the entire canon of Buddhist scriptures.
c 1100	Sei Shonagon writes her Pillow Book.

1111	China's 12 most eminent doctors compile a medical encyclopedia.
1127-1279	Southern Song dynasty
1173-1212	Life of Honen, Japanese founder of the Jodo, or Pure Land sect of Buddhism, which concentrates on the power of Amida to offer salvation.
1185	The Japanese Minamoto clan defeats the Taira clan at the sea-battle of Dan-no-ura.
1185-1333	Japanese Kamakura period
1191	Zen Buddhism is brought to Japan by the monk Eisai, who also introduces tea from China.
1192	Minamoto Yoritomo becomes Shogun, a permanent position of absolute military authority in Japan.
c 1200	Zen Buddhism is introduced to Japan.
13th century	Buddhism enters Mongolia.

1206-1368	Yuan (Mongol) dynasty
1210	Genghis Khan invades and conquers most of China.
1263	Kublai Khan moves his capital from Karakorum to Beijing, and begins a period of dialogue with Europe.
1274	Kublai Khan attempts to invade Japan.
1281	Kublai Khan's second attempt to invade Japan is prevented when the Mongol fleet is destroyed by a typhoon, or kamikaze (divine wind), thought by the Japanese to be sent by Amaterasu.
1287	Mongol forces destroy the Burmese capital of Pagan.
1333	The Kamakura Shogunate is overthrown.
1338-1568	Japanese Ashikaga period
c 1340	Rebellions against Mongol rule in China, and the rise of the White Lotus society, whose members believe that Maitreya, the future Buddha, is about to appear.
1368-1644	Ming dynasty
15th century	The Ba Xian are credited with immortality.
1402	Foundation of Malacca on the Malay Peninsula. As it develops into the major entrepôt of Southeast Asia, its population of Muslim traders spread Islam throughout the region.
1431	Thai seige of Angkor: Cambodians abandon the city and found a new capital at Phnom Penh.
1467-1568	Japanese Sengoku period
1467-1477	Onin War in Japan, over the shogunal succession, destroys much of Kyoto and begins a century of war between Japanese rival factions.
16th century	Guan Gong, a 3rd-century Chinese general, is deified as Guan Di, Daoist patron deity of soldiers and policemen.
1542	Arrival of the Portuguese in Japan.
1549	Francis Xavier arrives in Japan.

1568-1582	Rule of Japanese warlord Oda Nobunaga.
1569	Nobunaga licenses Jesuits to preach in Kyoto.
1571	Buddhist monastic establishment of Enryakuji is destroyed on the orders of Nobunaga.
1582-1598	Rule of Toyotomi Hideyoshi, who makes Osaka capital and completes reunification of Japan.
1592	Japanese invade Korea.
1592	Wu Cheng-en publishes a definitive version of the 14th-century story Journey to the West.
1597	Japanese attempt to invade Korea a second time.
1598-1616	Rule of Tokugawa Ieyasu, who establishes the Shogunate in 1603. Edo (Tokyo) becomes the capital of Japan.
1603-1868	Japanese Tokugawa period
17th century	Islam is dominant religion of South-east Asia.
17th century	The Shichi Fukujin are grouped as an assembly of Japanese immortals.
1609	Dutch merchants are allowed to trade at Nagasaki.
1612	Christian missionaries are expelled from Japan.
1638	Christian rebellion at Shimabara in Japan.
1640	Japan issues seclusion and exclusion edicts, ending trade with Europe.
1644-1912	Qing (Manchu) dynasty
1689	Sino-Russian Treaty of Nerchinsk, China's first-ever treaty with a European power.
1716-1745	Rule of Tokugawa Yoshimune, last effective Japanese shogun.
19th century	Siberian Shamanism declines in face of opposition from Russian Orthodox missionaries.
1839-1842	Opium War, and British occupation of Hong Kong.
1854	American naval expedition to Japan forces the Japanese to sign a treaty ending their policy of isolation.

1867	Tokugawa Shogunate overthrown.
1868	Meiji restoration: new Japanese imperial government established at Tokyo.
1871-1876	Japanese government is centralized and caste privileges ended.
1877	Japanese Satsuma Rebellion.
1889	Meiji Constitution established in Japan.
1894-1895	Sino-Japanese War.
1900	Chinese Boxer Rebellion.
1904-1905	Russo-Japanese War
1912	Chinese Revolution.
20th century	Siberian Shamans persecuted by Communists during Soviet period.
1949-	People's Republic of China
1970s	Excavations on Mount Li near Xian in China reveal tomb of first emperor, Qin Shihuang Di, with army of 7,500 terracotta guards.

INDEX

Page numbers in **bold** refer to illustrations

A

Abaasy 14, 71
Aizen Myoo 14, **14**
Altaic people 26, 38–9, 46, 71
Amaterasu 14–15, **15**, 16, 32, 33, **35**, 38, 39, 52–3, 55, 64–5, 70, 72
Ame-No-Uzume 15, **15**
Amida 16, **16**, 62
Amitabha 16, 44, 62
Amur people 46
Animals, shamanism **51**
Antaboga 16, 18
Ara 16, 37
As-Iga 16
Avalokiteshvara 44

B

Ba Xian 16–17, **17**, 42, **42–3**
Bagobo people 29, 56
Bagua **24**
Bajang 18
Bali (island) 16, 18, 60–1, 62
Barong 18, 60, **75**
Basuki 18
Batara Guru 18, 20, 52
Batara Kala 16, 18, 19, 62

Bedawang 16, 18–19
Benkei **18**, 19, 79
Benten 19, **19**, 63, 66, **66**
Bishamon 20, **20**, 63, 66, **66**
Bodhisattvas 22
Borneo 16, 34, 36, 37, 39, 46, 60, 61, 64
Boru Deak Parudjar 18, 20
Bota Ili 20–1, 72
Budaishi 33
Buddha 40, 52
Buddhism 42, 58, 66, 74
Bujaegn Yed 21, 79
Buriat people 26, 68
Buzhou, Mount 29

C

Cao Guojiu 17, **42**
Chewong people 21, 79
China 34, 58, 82
Chiyou 21, 60
City God 21, **21**
Confucianism 78
Creation myths 34, **34–5**

D

Daikoku **22**, 63, 66, **67**
Dainichi-Nyorai 22, **23**, 28
Daoism 16, 24, 41, 42, 44, 46, 57, 61, 64, 65, 66, 69, 72, 76, 78, 79, 81, 82, 84
Dayak people 16, 22, 36, 37, 39, 46, 61
Demong 22
Demons 74, **74–5**
Didis Mahendera 22, 36, 39, 61
Diya 22
Dizang Wang 22
Dongyue Dadi 22–3, 80
Dragons **25**, 58, **58–9**
Drumming, shamans **50**

E

Earth God 23, **23**
Ebisu 23, 63, 66, **67**
Ec 23, 41
"Eight Immortals" 16–17, 42, **42–3**
Emma-O 26, **26**, 56

Erlik 26, 46, 71
Es 26
Esege Malan Tengri 26
Evenk people 46

F

Fangchang 57
Fu Xi 26–7, **27**, **35**, 54, 63
Fudo-Myoo 28, **28**
Fugen-Bosatsu 28, **28**
Fukurokuju 28–9, **29**, 63, **67**
Fuxing 62

G

Ganesha 64
Gao Yao 29, **29**
Gautama Buddha 41, 52
Gimokodan 29
Gong-Gong 29
Guan Di 30, **30**
Guanyin 30–1, **31**, 44
Guardian Kings 20
Guei 31

H

Hachiman 32, **32**
Han dynasty 62
Han Xiang 17, **43**
Han Zhongli 17
He Xiangu 17, **42**
Hell **75**
Heng Shan, Mount 82, **83**
Hikohohodemi 32–3, **33**, 39, 53
Hinduism 66
Hinkon 33
Hkun Ai 33
Honosuseri 32, 33
Hotei 33, **33**, 63, 66, **67**
Hua Shan 82, **83**
Huang Di 21, 36, **36**, 60, 63, **63**, 65, 73, **83**
Hui-Neng **59**

I

Iban people 16, 22, 34, 37, 60, 64

Ida-Ten 36

Ila-Ilai Langit 36, 39

Inari 36–7, **37**, 70, 74

Indonesia 72

Irik 16, 37

Issun Boshi 37

Itchita 37

Izanagi 14, 23, **34**, 38, **38**, 40, 64, 70, 79

Izanami 14, 23, **34**, 38, **38**, 40, 64, 79

J

"Jade Emperor" 21, 22–3, 46, 48, 52, 61,

65, 72, 73, 80–1, 82

Jar-Sub 38–9

Jata 36, 39

Jigoku 26

Jigokudayu **74**

Jimmu-Tenno 33, 39, **39**, 53

Jizo-Bosatzu 39, **39**

Journey to the West 30

Jurojin 29, 40, **40**, 63, **67**

K

Kadaklan 40

Kagutsuchi 38, 40

Kami 40

Kappa 40, **40**

Kedang people 20, 72

Ket people 26, 70

Khadau 46

Khori Tumed 40–1

Khosadam 23, 41

Kishimo-Jin 41

Kunlun 41, **41**, 84

Kwannon 30, 44, **44**

L

Lan Caihe 17, **43**

Lao Jun 44, **45**, 61, 81

Laos 69

Laozi 61, 81

Lei Gong 26–7, 44–5, **45**, 46

Li Jing 52, **53**

Li Tieguai 16, 17, **42**, 73

Lightning Goddess 46, **46**, 60

Ling Zhi 46, 47, 57

Long Wang 46, **46**, 58

Losy 56

Lu Dongbin 17, **43**

Luxing 62

M

Ma'Betisek people 49

Magyar people 72

Mahatala 36, 39, 46

Maidere 26, 46, 71

Main 46

O

Ojin, Emperor 32

Okuninushi 23, 53, 55, **55**, 64, 70, 76

Omito Fu 16

Oni 37, 56, **56**, 74, **74**

Oribe Shima 70

Ostyak people 16

Ot 56, 71

Otshirvani 56

P

Pagodas **83**

Pamalak Bagobo 56

Pangu 34, **35**, 56–7, **56**, **57**, 82

Pei Tou Immortals **25**

Peng Lai 57

Philippines 29, 40, 56

Phoenix **25**

Polong 57

Pudai 60, **60**

Pulang Gana 60

Pure Land 16, 62

Q

Qing dynasty 30

Qormusta 60

R

Radin 60

Rain Spirit 60, **60**

Rangda 18, 60–1, **60**, **75**

Rowang Riwo 22, 36, 39, 61

S

Samoyed people 52, 54

San Guan Dadi 61, **61**

San Qing Daozu 61, **61**

San Xing 62, **62**, 64

Semara 16, 62

Sengalong Burong 64

Sesha 52

Setesuyara 16, 18, 19, 62

Shaka-Nyorai 62, **63**

Shamans 40, 50, **50–1**, 68

Shang Di 63

Malaysia 79

Mamaldi 46

Manuk Manuk 34, 46

Marishi-Ten 46

Men Shen 48, **48**

Minamoto clan 79

Mindanao 29

Miroku **49**

Miroku-Bosatsu 48

Momotaro 48, **49**, 56

Mongolia 40, 50, 56, 68

Monju-Bosatsu 48–9, **49**

"Monkey King" 30, 76

Mountains, sacred 82, **82–3**

Moyang Kapir 49

Moyang Melur 49

Mucilinda 52, **52**

N

Naga Padoha 18, 20, 52

Nagas 52, **52**, **75**

Naraka 74

Nazha 52, **53**

Nga 52, 54

Ninigi 15, 32, 33, 52–3, 55

Nio 54, **54**

Nu Gua 26–7, 29, 54, **54**

Num 52, 54

Shang dynasty 63

Shen Nong 21, 63, **63**

Shichi Fukujin 19, 20, 22, 23, 28, 33, 40, 63, 66, **66–7**

Shinto 14, 32, 33, 36, 38, 40, 53, 55, 64, 66, 70, 72, 79

Shiva 18, 20, 52

Shoten 64

Shotoku, Prince 20

Shou Lao **43**, 62, 64, **64**

Shouxing 62

Shun 64, 73, 78

Siberia 14, 26, 33, 37, 38–9, 41, 46, 52, 54, 56, 68, 70, 71, 72

Song Shan, Mount 82, **83**

Suku-Na-Bikona 64

Sumatra 18, 34, 46

Surong Gunting 64

Susano-Wo 14–15, **35**, 37, 38, 53, 55, 64–5, 70, 72

Suseri-Hime 55

T

Tai Shan 82, **82**

Tai Sui 65, **65**

Taiyi 65

Taiyi Tianzun 65

Tang dynasty 48

Tarvaa 68

Tawara-Toda 68

Tengri 68

Tengu 19, 68, **69**, 79

Tenkai 63

Tevne 68–9

Thailand 34, 69

Thens 69

Ti-Ts'ang Wang 22

Tian 69, **69**, 76

Tian-Long 22

Tinguian people 40

Tokoyo 70, **70**

Tomam 70

Tsukiyomi 14, 37, 38, 64, 70

Tung Hkam 33

Tungu people 33

Turkic people 38–9, 56, 71

U

Uke-Mochi 37, 65, 70–1

Ulgan 26, 46, 71

Ulu Toyo'n 14, 71

Umai 56, 71

Urashima 71, **71**

V

Vishnu 52

Vizi-Ember 72

W

Wakahiru-Me 72

Wata Rian 20–1, 72

Wen Chang 22, 62, 72, **72**

Wind God 72–3, **72**

Wu Di 73

X

Xi-He 73, 78

Xi Wang Mu 16, 30, 41, 73, **73**, 78, 81, 84

Xia dynasty 80

Xian 57, 76, **76**

Xuan Zang 76, **77**

Y

Yakami 55, 76

Yakushi-Nyorai 22, 76, **77**

Yakut people 14, 37, 50, 71

Yama 26

Yamato Takeru 76–7

Yang see Yin and yang

Yanluo Wang 26, 30, 78, **78**

Yao 29, 64, 73, 78–9, **79**

"Yellow Emperor" 36, 65, 73, 78

Yenisei people 23, 41

Yi 73, 78–9, 84–5

Yin and yang 24, **24–5**, 31, 34, 56–7, 61, 73, 78, 79

Yingzhou 57

Yinlugen Bud 21, 79

Yomi 14, 38, 79

Yoshitsune 19, 79, **79**

Yu 80, **80**

Yu Di 80

Yu Huang 21, 22–3, 46, 48, 52, 61, 73, 80–1, **80**, **81**, 82, 84

Yuqiang 81, **81**

Yurak people 52, 54

Z

Zao Jun 84, **84**

Zhang E 73, 78–9, 84

Zhang Guolao 17, **43**

Zhang Lang 84

Zhong-li Quan 16–17, **43**

Zhu Rong 29

Picture Acknowledgments

The Publishers are grateful to the agencies listed below for kind permission to reproduce the following images in this book.

AKG, London: p31 National Museum, Beijing. Ancient Art and Architecture: p20; p22b; p28br; p30tl; p32; p40tl; p43tr; p44r; p49tr; p52tl; p52tr; p54t; p63tl; p63bl; p65t; p66tr; p66m; p68; p77b. Duncan Baird Publishing/Japanese Gallery, London: p38. Bildarchiv Foto, Marburg: p41b. Bridgeman Art Library: p37 Chris Beetles Gallery, London; p39tl Victoria & Albert Museum, London; p44l Blackburn Museum and Art Gallery; p56t private collection; p60br Museum für Völkerkunder, Basle. The British Museum: p35tl; p45b. Christie's Art Gallery: p16; p19; p22t; p26tl; p26tr; p29l; p29tr; p33b; p42b; p43bm; p43br; p47b; p58t; p59tl; p59tr; p62bl; p66b; p67tl; p67tr; p67br; p67bm; p67bl; p72t; p76tr. Corbis: p52b Luca I. Tettoni; p12/13 and p73 Pierre Colombel; p14 Sakamoto Photo Research Laboratory; p15tl Asian Art & Archaeology, Inc.; p25br Asian Art & Archaeology, Inc.; p28tl Sakamoto Photo Research Laboratory; p28tr Sakamoto Photo Research Laboratory; p34 Ric Ergenbright; p41t Keren Su; p46b Adam Woolfitt; p49b Sakamoto Photo Research Laboratory; p51t Christel Gerstenberg; p55 Macduff Everton; p60t Keren Su; p62tr Kimbell Art Museum; p69 Royal Ontario Museum; p71 Asian Art & Archaeology, Inc.; p74b Asian Art & Archaeology, Inc.; p75t Jack Fields; p75br Michael Freeman; p75bt Morton Beebe, S.F.; p76tl Asian Art & Archaeology, Inc.; p78 Royal Ontario Museum; p81t Brian Vikander; p82t Lowell Georgia; p82b Lowell Georgia; p83tr Lowell Georgia; p83mr Keren Su; p83b Keren Su. CM Dixon: p30br; p42t; p43tl; p62tl; p64; p84. ET Archive: p25tl; p35b; p45tl British Museum, p45tr British Museum; p58b; p79t; p84. Mary Evans: p24b; p25tr; p39br; p43bl; p51b; p59b; p74r. Michael Holford: p24t. Icorec: p56b. National Palace Museum, Taipei: p79b; p81b. K Stevens: p17; p21; p23t; p46t; p47t; p48tr; p48tl; p53r; p53l; p54b; p57; p60bl; p61tr; p61tl; p61br; p61bm; p61bl; p65b; p72b; p77t; p80b; p80t.